McGraw-Hill's

FRENCH
PICTURE DICTIONARY

McGraw·Hill

New York   Chicago   San Francisco   Lisbon   London   Madrid   Mexico City
Milan   New Delhi   San Juan   Seoul   Singapore   Sydney   Toronto

Welcome to our picture dictionary!
Here's an exciting way for you to learn French words and phrases that will help you talk about the world around you. This dictionary is fun to use—look at all the things you can do:

I CAN SEE . . .
French words that begin with A, or with BR, or with . . .

COLORS AND SHAPES
Find the objects colored . . . Are there any round objects?

SYLLABLES
Clap your hands as many times as the syllables of the words:
le ta-pis; **la té-lé-vi-sion**

TELLING THE DIFFERENCES
What is the difference between **la brosse** and **le plumeau**? What do they have in common?

DRAWINGS
Does **la sauris** have a tail? Does **la clé** have a hole?

SIZES
Which is the biggest object? And which is the smallest?

WHAT ARE THEY DOING?
Can you say what the baby is doing? And what about the girl?

In the living room
Dans la salle de séjour

CEILING **LE PLAFOND**

CORNER **LE CO**

DOOR **LA PORTE**

PAINTINGS **LES TABLEAUX**

PORTRAIT **LE PORTRAIT**

LANDSCAPE **LE PAYSAGE**

BLINDS **LA PERSIENNE**

CUSHION **LE COUSSIN**

TELEVISION **LA TÉLÉVISION**

IRONING BOARD **LA PLANCHE À REPASSER**

BROOM **LA BROSSE**

VACUUM **L'ASPIRATEUR**

LAUNDRY BASKET **LA CUVETT**

VASE **LE VASE**

FRAME **LE CADR**

CLOTH **LE CHIFFON**

LAMP **LA LAMPE**

CANDLEHOLDER **LE CANDÉLABRE**

SEARCH AND FIND

Find all these things in the picture on the left.

You will notice that almost all the French words in this book have **le**, **la**, **l'**, or **les** before them. These words simply mean "the" and are usually used when you talk about things in French.

At the back of this book you will find a French-English Glossary and an English-French Glossary, where you can look up words in alphabetical order and find out exactly where they are located in the book. There is also pronunciation help so that you can say each French word correctly.

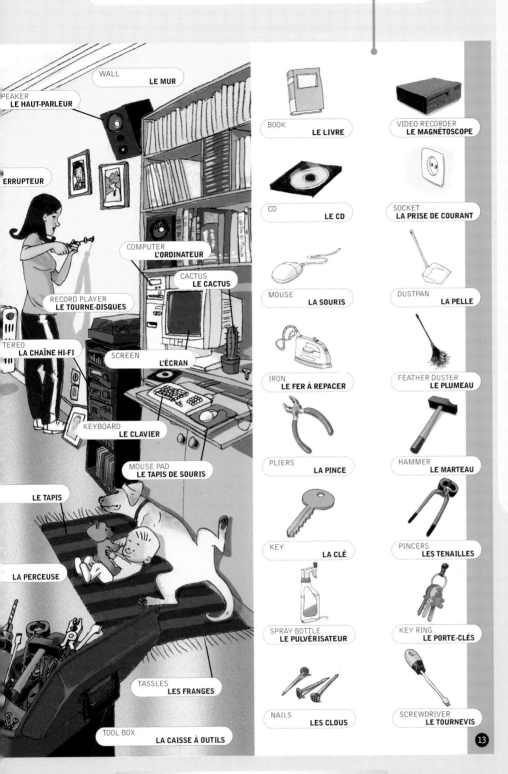

WALL **LE MUR**

PEAKER **LE HAUT-PARLEUR**

ERRUPTEUR

COMPUTER **L'ORDINATEUR**

CACTUS **LE CACTUS**

RECORD PLAYER **LE TOURNE-DISQUES**

TEREO **LA CHAÎNE HI-FI**

SCREEN **L'ÉCRAN**

KEYBOARD **LE CLAVIER**

MOUSE PAD **LE TAPIS DE SOURIS**

LE TAPIS

LA PERCEUSE

TASSLES **LES FRANGES**

TOOL BOX **LA CAISSE À OUTILS**

BOOK **LE LIVRE**

CD **LE CD**

MOUSE **LA SOURIS**

IRON **LE FER À REPACER**

PLIERS **LA PINCE**

KEY **LA CLÉ**

SPRAY BOTTLE **LE PULVÉRISATEUR**

NAILS **LES CLOUS**

VIDEO RECORDER **LE MAGNÉTOSCOPE**

SOCKET **LA PRISE DE COURANT**

DUSTPAN **LA PELLE**

FEATHER DUSTER **LE PLUMEAU**

HAMMER **LE MARTEAU**

PINCERS **LES TENAILLES**

KEY RING **LE PORTE-CLÉS**

SCREWDRIVER **LE TOURNEVIS**

13

WHERE ARE THEY?

Is **la persienne** near the girl? And who has **le tournevis**?

WHAT IS IT USED FOR?

What is **le clavier** used for? What bout **l'aspirateur**?

Previously published under the original title: *DICOMAGES: Dictionnaire en images*. Copyright © Marcelo Pérez—Ediciones SM, 2001. All rights reserved. Published by arrangement with Ediciones SM.

ISBN 0-07-142813-5

TABLE OF CONTENTS • TABLE DES MATIÈRES

At home
À la maison

At school
À l'école

The family
La famille

ROLLER BLIND
LE STORE

CLOCK
LA PENDULE

BAG
LE SA

PRESENT
LE CADEAU

GRANDFATHER
LE GRAND-PÈR

BALLOONS
LES BALLONS

MOTHER
LA MÈRE

SISTER
LA SŒUR

FATHER
LE PÈRE

BROTHER
LE FRÈRE

GRANDMOTHER
LA GRAND-MÈRE

PLANT
LA PLANTE

BABY
LE BÉBÉ

UNCLE
L'ONCLE

CAKE
LA TARTE

NAPKIN
LA SERVIETTE

DRINKING STRAW
LA PAILLE

PAPER STREAMER
LE SERPENTIN

TABLECLOTH
LA NAPPE

6

NEIGHBOR **LE VOISIN**

AUNT **LA TANTE**

NEIGHBOR **LA VOISINE**

COUSIN **LE COUSIN**

DOUGHNUT **LA GIMBLETTE**

CANDLE **LA BOUGIE**

ICE **LE GLAÇON**

CHERRY **LA CERISE**

SANDWICH **LE SANDWICH**

MATCHES **LES ALLUMETTES**

SANDWICH **LE SANDWICH**

TOOTHPICKS **LES CURE-DENTS**

SALTSHAKER **LA SALIÈRE**

MASK **LE MASQUE**

NOISEMAKER **LA LANGUE DE BELLE-MÈRE**

CROWN **LA COURONNE**

PITCHER **LA CARAFE**

BOTTLE **LA BOUTEILLE**

HAIR **LES CHEVEUX**

GLASS **LE VERRE**

POCKET **LA POCHE**

RANGE HOOD **L'EXTRACTEUR**

MICROWAVE **LE FOUR MICRO-ONDES**

SPICE RACK **LES ÉPICES**

SAUCEPAN **LE POÊLON**

CUTTING BOARD **LA PLANCHE À COUPER**

A PIECE OF TOAST **LE TOAST**

JUICE **LE JUS**

OVEN **LE FO**

JARS **LES POTS**

BIB **LE BAVOUR**

LID **LE COUVERCLE**

CEREAL **LES CÉRÉALES**

HIGH CHAIR **LE CHASE-BÉBÉ**

BOWL **LE BOL**

CARTON **LA BRIQUE**

TRAY **LE PLATEAU**

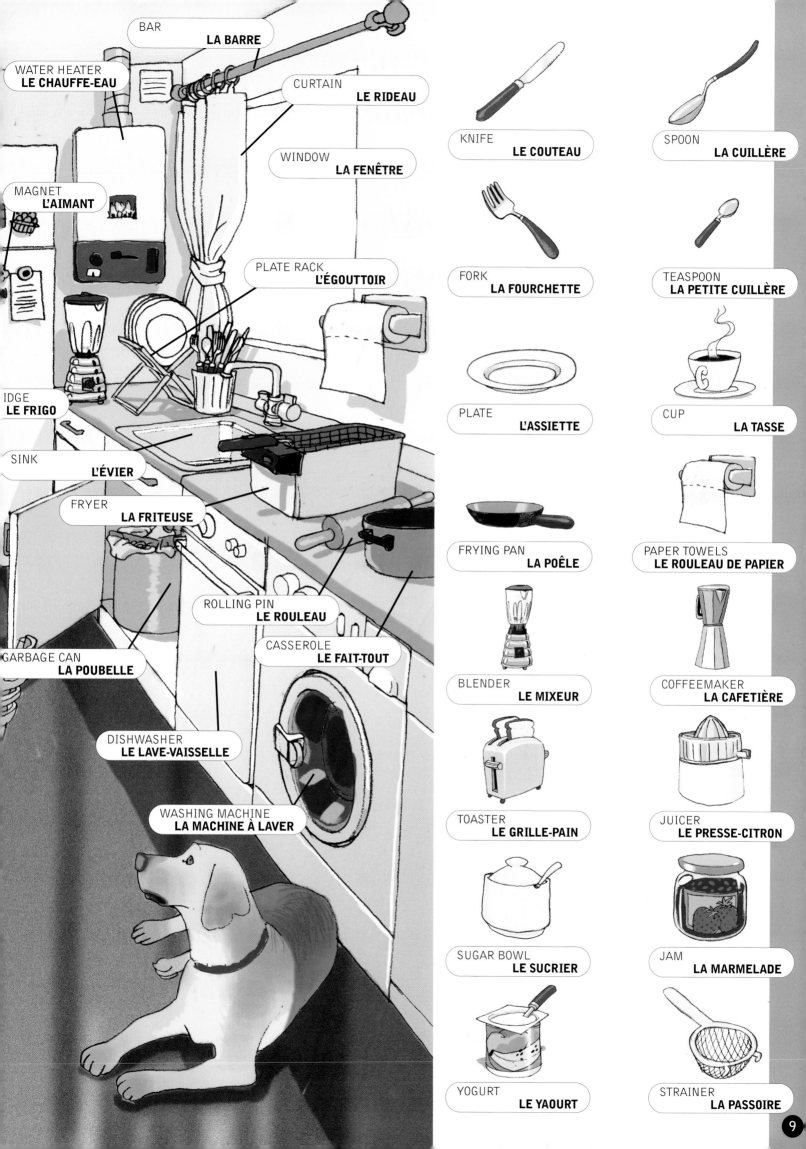

BAR
LA BARRE

WATER HEATER
LE CHAUFFE-EAU

CURTAIN
LE RIDEAU

WINDOW
LA FENÊTRE

MAGNET
L'AIMANT

PLATE RACK
L'ÉGOUTTOIR

IDGE
LE FRIGO

SINK
L'ÉVIER

FRYER
LA FRITEUSE

ROLLING PIN
LE ROULEAU

CASSEROLE
LE FAIT-TOUT

GARBAGE CAN
LA POUBELLE

DISHWASHER
LE LAVE-VAISSELLE

WASHING MACHINE
LA MACHINE À LAVER

KNIFE
LE COUTEAU

SPOON
LA CUILLÈRE

FORK
LA FOURCHETTE

TEASPOON
LA PETITE CUILLÈRE

PLATE
L'ASSIETTE

CUP
LA TASSE

FRYING PAN
LA POÊLE

PAPER TOWELS
LE ROULEAU DE PAPIER

BLENDER
LE MIXEUR

COFFEEMAKER
LA CAFETIÈRE

TOASTER
LE GRILLE-PAIN

JUICER
LE PRESSE-CITRON

SUGAR BOWL
LE SUCRIER

JAM
LA MARMELADE

YOGURT
LE YAOURT

STRAINER
LA PASSOIRE

LETTUCE • **LA LAITUE**

TOMATO • **LA TOMATE**

ONION • **L'OIGNON**

GARLIC • **L'AIL**

CARROT • **LA CAROTTE**

PEAS • **LES PETITS POIS**

BEANS •
LES HARICOTS VERTS

ZUCCHINI • **LA COURGETTE**

LEEK • **LE POIREAU**

TURNIP • **LE NAVET**

POTATO •
LA POMME DE TERRE

CHARD • **LES BLETTES**

ARTICHOKE • **L'ARTICHAUT**

PUMPKIN • **LA CITROUILLE**

GREEN PEPPER •
LE POIVRON VERT

RED PEPPER •
LE POIVRON ROUGE

GREEN ASPARAGUS •
LES ASPERGES VERTES

WHITE ASPARAGUS •
LES ASPERGES

ALMONDS •
LES AMANDES

HAZELNUTS •
LES NOISETTES

PEANUTS • **LES
CACAHOUÈTES**

PISTACHIO NUTS •
LES PISTACHES

CASHEW NUTS •
LES ANACARDES

BANANA • **LA BANANE**

ORANGE • **L'ORANGE**

LEMON • **LE CITRON**

GRAPEFRUIT •
LE PAMPLEMOUSSE

APPLE • **LA POMME**

PEACH • **LA PÊCHE**

APRICOT • **L'ABRICOT**

MEDLAR • **LA NÈFLE**

PEAR • **LA POIRE**

MANGO • **LA MANGUE**

AVOCADO • **L'AVOCAT**

KIWI • **LE KIWI**

MELON • **LE MELON**

PINEAPPLE • **L'ANANAS**

COCONUT • **LA NOIX DE COCO**

WATERMELON• **LA
PASTÈQUE**

WALNUTS • **LES NOIX**

STRAWBERRIES • **LES FRAISES**

GRAPES • **LES
RAISINS**

RAISINS• **LES RAISINS SECS**

In the living room
Dans la salle de séjour

CEILING **LE PLAFOND**

CORNER **LE COIN**

DOOR **LA PORTE**

PAINTINGS **LES TABLEAUX**

PORTRAIT **LE PORTRAIT**

LANDSCAPE **LE PAYSAGE**

BLINDS **LA PERSIENNE**

TELEVISION **LA TÉLÉVISION**

CUSHION **LE COUSSIN**

IRONING BOARD **LA PLANCHE À REPASSER**

BROOM **LA BROSSE**

VACUUM **L'ASPIRATEUR**

LAUNDRY BASKET **LA CUVETTE**

VASE **LE VASE**

FRAME **LE CADRE**

CLOTH **LE CHIFFON**

LAMP **LA LAMPE**

CANDLEHOLDER **LE CANDÉLABRE**

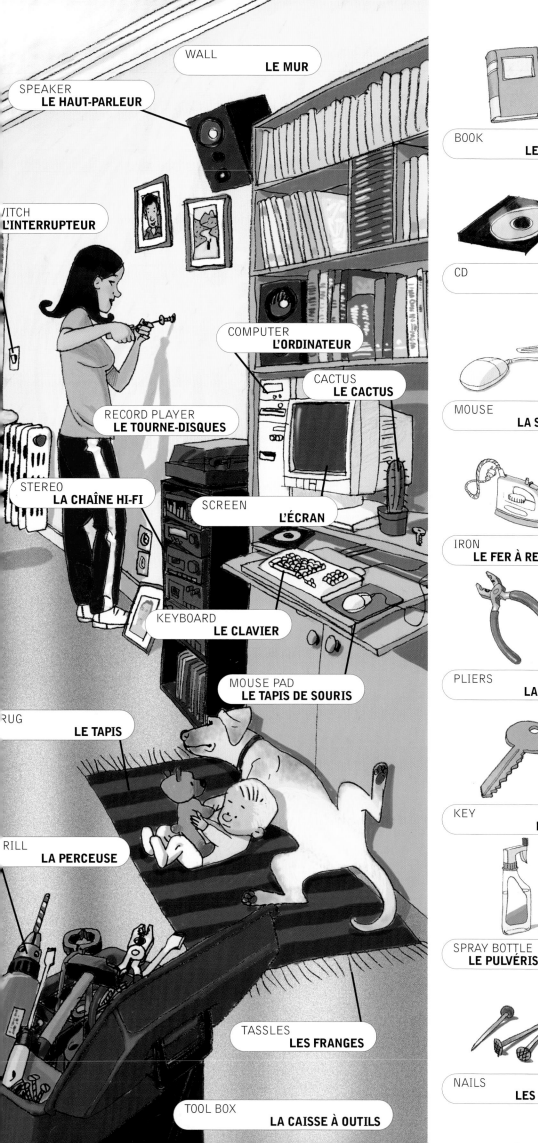

SPEAKER
LE HAUT-PARLEUR

WALL
LE MUR

SWITCH
L'INTERRUPTEUR

COMPUTER
L'ORDINATEUR

CACTUS
LE CACTUS

RECORD PLAYER
LE TOURNE-DISQUES

STEREO
LA CHAÎNE HI-FI

SCREEN
L'ÉCRAN

KEYBOARD
LE CLAVIER

MOUSE PAD
LE TAPIS DE SOURIS

RUG
LE TAPIS

DRILL
LA PERCEUSE

TASSLES
LES FRANGES

TOOL BOX
LA CAISSE À OUTILS

BOOK
LE LIVRE

VIDEO RECORDER
LE MAGNÉTOSCOPE

CD
LE CD

SOCKET
LA PRISE DE COURANT

MOUSE
LA SOURIS

DUSTPAN
LA PELLE

IRON
LE FER À REPACER

FEATHER DUSTER
LE PLUMEAU

PLIERS
LA PINCE

HAMMER
LE MARTEAU

KEY
LA CLÉ

PINCERS
LES TENAILLES

SPRAY BOTTLE
LE PULVÉRISATEUR

KEY RING
LE PORTE-CLÉS

NAILS
LES CLOUS

SCREWDRIVER
LE TOURNEVIS

CHAIR • **LA CHAISE**

ARMCHAIR • **LE FAUTEUIL**

ROCKING CHAIR •
LE FAUTEUIL À BASCULE

ARMCHAIR • **LE FAUTEU**

SOFA • **LE CANAPÉ**

DIVAN • **LE DIVAN**

OTTOMAN • **LE POUF**

DINING TABLE • **LA TABLE**

ROUND TABLE • **LA TABLE RONDE**

DESK • **LE BUREAU**

HUTCH •
LE GARDE-MANGER

DISPLAY CABINET •
LA VITRINE

SIDEBOARD• **LE BUFFET**

BED • **LE LIT**

CRIB • **LE BERCEAU**

BOOKCASE • **LA BIBLIOTHÈQUE**

ARMOIRE • **L'ARMOIRE**

DRESSER • **LA COMMODE**

DESK • **LE SECRÉTAIRE**

DRESSING TABLE •
LA COIFFEUSE

In the bathroom
Dans la salle de bains

PARTITION
LE PANNEAU COUL

RADIO
LE POSTE DE RADIO

COLOGNE
L'EAU DE COLOGNE

STEAM
LA VAPEUR

SHOWER
LA DOUCHE

SHOWER GEL
LE GEL

SHAMPOO
LE SHAMPOING

PERFUME
LE PARFUM

MEDICINE CABINET
LA BOÎTE À PHARMACIE

TOILET PAPER
LE PAPIER HYGIÉNIQUE

BATHTUB
LA BAIGNOIRE

BATHROBE
LE PIEGNOIR

TOILET
LES CABINETS

BIDET
LE BIDET

STOOL
LE TABOURET

SCALE
LA BALANCE

TILES
LES DALLES

MIRROR
LE MIROIR

DEODORANT
LE DÉODORANT

INK
LE LAVABO

TOWEL
LA SERVIETTE DE BAIN

KNOB
LA POIGNÉE

FAUCET
LE ROBINET

PLUG
LE BOUCHON

SOAP
LE SAVON

SPONGE
L'ÉPONGE

LIPSTICK
LE ROUGE À LÈVRES

COTTON SWABS
LES COTONS-TIGES

HAIR DRYER
LE SÉCHOIR

TALCUM POWDER
LE TALC

TOOTHPASTE
LE DENTIFRICE

TOOTHBRUSH
LA BROSSE À DENTS

RAZOR
LE RASOIR

NAILBRUSH
LA BROSSE À ONGLES

COMB
LE PEIGNE

HAIRBRUSH
LA BROSSE À CHEVEUX

POTTY
LE VASE DE NUIT

TISSUES
LES MOUCHOIRS EN PAPIER

ARM
LE BRAS

BELLY BUTTON
LE NOMBRIL

BREAST/CHEST
LA POITRINE

LEG
LA JAMBE

HAND
LA MAIN

ANKLE
LA CHEVILLE

FOOT
LE PIED

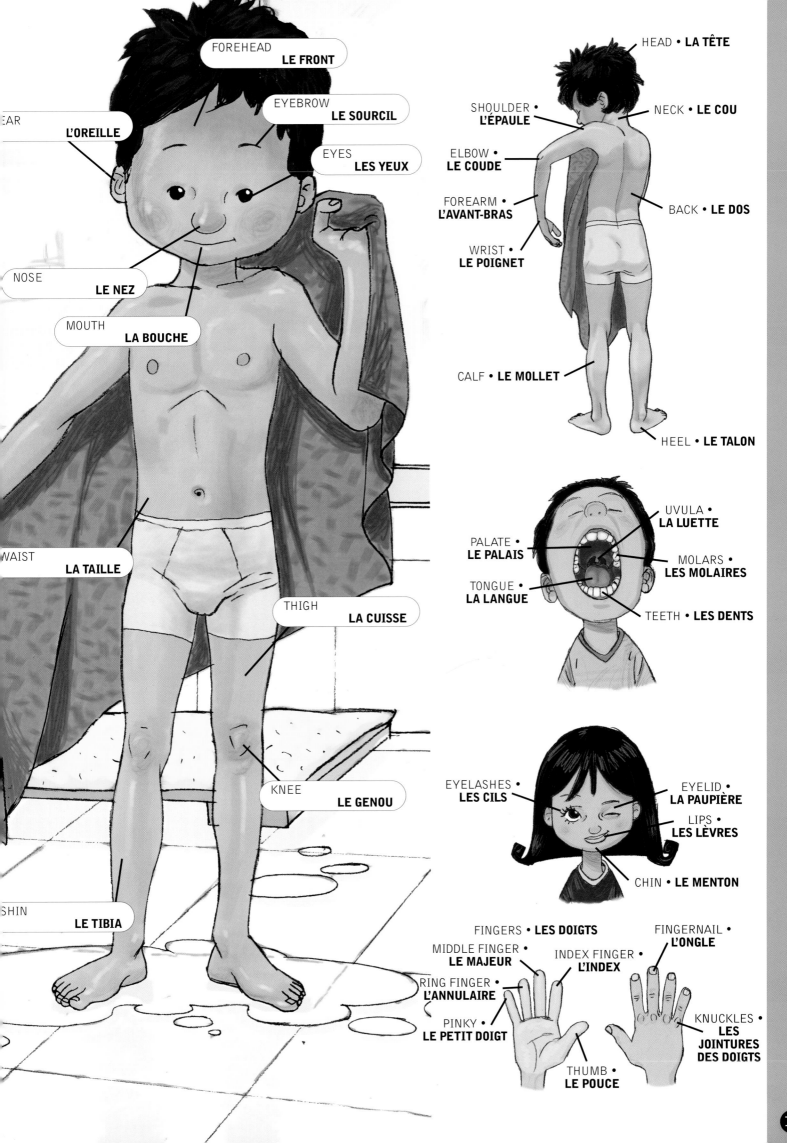

FOREHEAD **LE FRONT**

EYEBROW **LE SOURCIL**

EYES **LES YEUX**

EAR

L'OREILLE

NOSE

LE NEZ

MOUTH **LA BOUCHE**

WAIST **LA TAILLE**

THIGH **LA CUISSE**

KNEE **LE GENOU**

SHIN **LE TIBIA**

HEAD • **LA TÊTE**

SHOULDER • **L'ÉPAULE**

NECK • **LE COU**

ELBOW • **LE COUDE**

FOREARM • **L'AVANT-BRAS**

BACK • **LE DOS**

WRIST • **LE POIGNET**

CALF • **LE MOLLET**

HEEL • **LE TALON**

UVULA • **LA LUETTE**

PALATE • **LE PALAIS**

MOLARS • **LES MOLAIRES**

TONGUE • **LA LANGUE**

TEETH • **LES DENTS**

EYELASHES • **LES CILS**

EYELID • **LA PAUPIÈRE**

LIPS • **LES LÈVRES**

CHIN • **LE MENTON**

FINGERS • **LES DOIGTS**

FINGERNAIL • **L'ONGLE**

MIDDLE FINGER • **LE MAJEUR**

INDEX FINGER • **L'INDEX**

RING FINGER • **L'ANNULAIRE**

PINKY • **LE PETIT DOIGT**

KNUCKLES • **LES JOINTURES DES DOIGTS**

THUMB • **LE POUCE**

In the bedroom
Dans la chambre

ROBOT
LE ROBOT

READING LAMP
LA LAMPE

BEDSPREAD
LE COUVRE-LIT

RACKET
LA RAQUETTE

LADDER
L'ECHELLE

POSTER
LE POSTER

TRUNK
LE COFFRE

PILLOW
L'OREILLER

COMFORTER
LA COUETTE

CRIB
LE BERCEAU

PAJAMAS
LE PYJAMA

DIAPER
LA COUCHE

BLANKET
LA COUVERTURE

SHEET
LE DRAP

MATTRESS
LE MATELAS

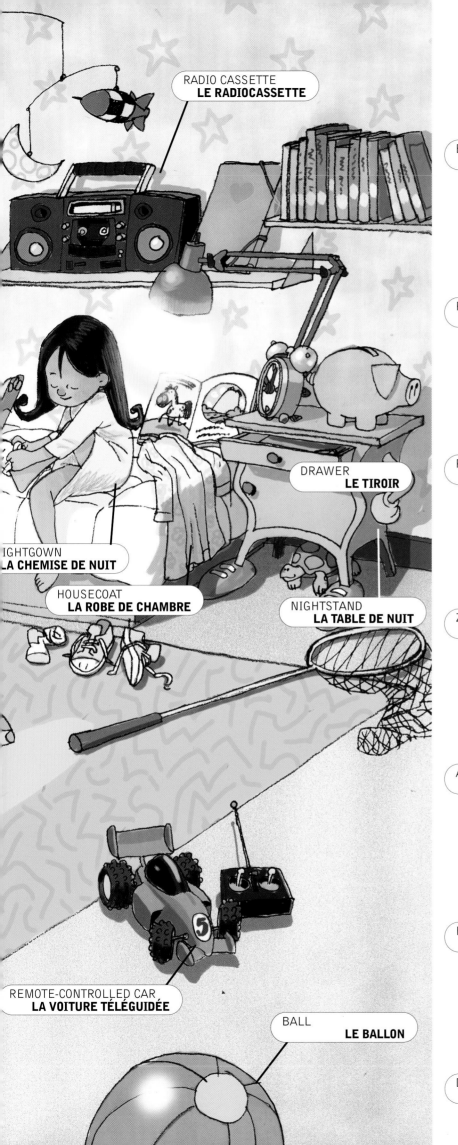

RADIO CASSETTE
LE RADIOCASSETTE

DRAWER
LE TIROIR

NIGHTGOWN
LA CHEMISE DE NUIT

HOUSECOAT
LA ROBE DE CHAMBRE

NIGHTSTAND
LA TABLE DE NUIT

REMOTE-CONTROLLED CAR
LA VOITURE TÉLÉGUIDÉE

BALL
LE BALLON

BOTTLE
LE BIBERON

PACIFIER
LA SUCETTE

RATTLE
LE HOCHET

BUTTON
LE BOUTON

PIGGY BANK
LA TIRELIRE

BUTTONHOLE
LA BOUTONNIÈRE

ZIPPER
LA FERMETURE ÉCLAIR

LACES
LES LACETS

ALARM CLOCK
LE RÉVEIL

STORYBOOK
LE CONTE

HANGER
LE PORTEMANTEAU

FOLDER
LA CHEMISE

DINOSAUR
LE DINOSAURE

DOLL
LE POUPON

PANTIES • **LA CULOTTE**   UNDERPANTS • **LE CALEÇON**   SOCKS • **LES CHAUSSETTES**   TIGHTS • **LE COLLANT**

T-SHIRT • **LE TEE-SHIRT**   KNITTED SHIRT • **LE POLO**   SHIRT • **LA CHEMISE**

CARDIGAN • **LA VESTE**   SWEATER • **LE PULL-OVER**   VEST• **LE GILET**

DRESS • **LA ROBE**   JUMPER • **LA ROBE CHASUBLE**   SKIRT • **LA JUPE**

SHORTS • **LE SHORT**

PANTS • **LE PANTALON**

OVERALLS • **LA SALOPETTE**

COAT • **LE MANTEAU**

JEAN JACKET • **LE BLOUSON**

RAINCOAT • **L'IMPERMÉABLE**

SHOES • **LES CHAUSSURES**

SNEAKERS • **LES BASKETS**

SANDALS • **LES SANDALES**

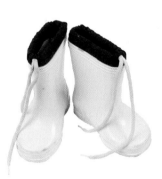

BOOTS • **LES BOTTES**

HAT • **LE BONNET**

SWIMMING TRUNKS • **LE MAILLOT DE BAIN**

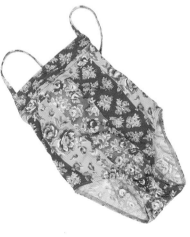

SWIMSUIT • **LE MAILLOT DE BAIN**

TO KISS
EMBRASSER

TO HUG
PRENDRE DANS SES BRAS

TO PET
CARESSER

TO LOOK AT
VOIR

TO LISTEN
ÉCOUTER

TO TASTE
DÉGUSTER

TO SMELL
SENTIR

TO TOUCH
TOUCHER

TO EAT
MANGER

TO DRINK
BOIRE

TO SERVE
SERVIR

TO COOK
CUISINER

TO SPREAD
ÉTALER

TO BREAK
ROMPRE

TO PEEL
ÉPLUCHER

TO WHISK
BATTRE

TO DO THE WASHING-UP
LAVER

TO BLOW
SOUFFLER

TO GIVE A PRESENT
FAIRE CADEAU

TO CLEAN
ÉPOUSSETER

TO SWEEP
BALAYER

TO MOP
NETTOYER

TO IRON
REPASSER

TO HANG UP
ÉTENDRE

TO TAKE A BATH
PRENDRE UN BAIN

TO DRY ONESELF
SE SÉCHER

TO BRUSH
BROSSER

TO GET DIRTY
SE SALIR

TO WASH ONESELF
SE LAVER

TO SHAVE
SE RASER

TO CUT ONE'S NAILS
SE COUPER LES ONGLES

TO GO TO BED
SE COUCHER

TO GET UP
SE LEVER

TO SLEEP
DORMIR

TO MAKE ONE'S BED
FAIRE SON LIT

TO STRETCH
S'ÉTIRER

TO YAWN
BÂILLER

TO COMB ONE'S HAIR
SE PEIGNER

TO GET DRESSED
S'HABILLER

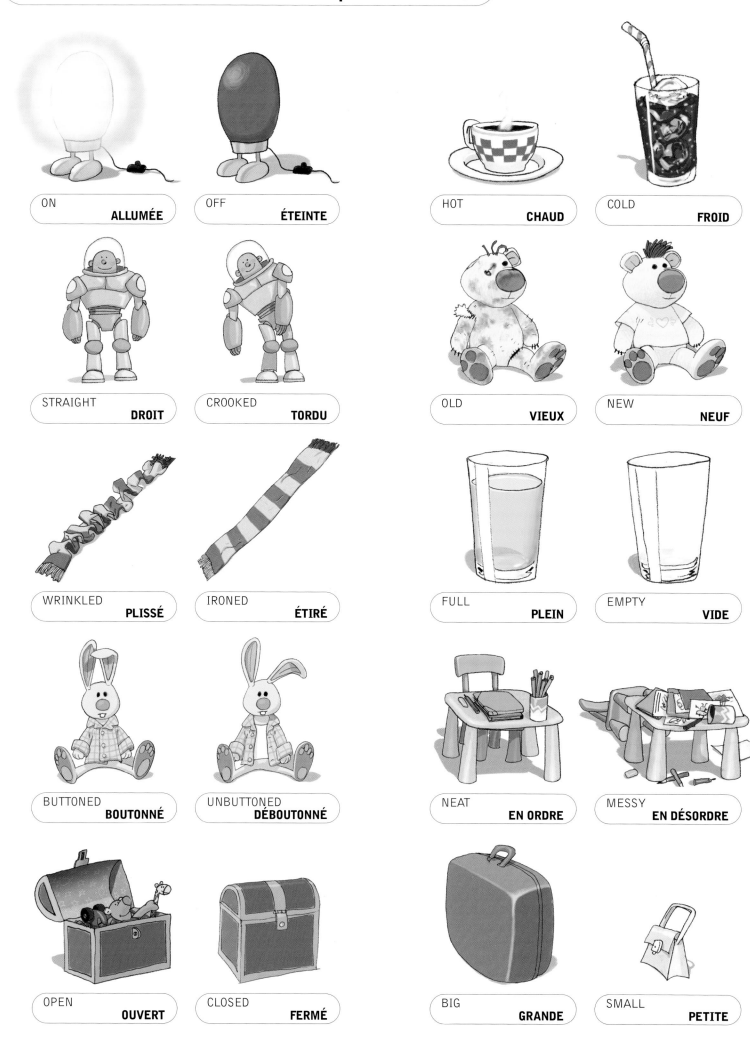

ON **ALLUMÉE**	OFF **ÉTEINTE**	HOT **CHAUD**	COLD **FROID**
STRAIGHT **DROIT**	CROOKED **TORDU**	OLD **VIEUX**	NEW **NEUF**
WRINKLED **PLISSÉ**	IRONED **ÉTIRÉ**	FULL **PLEIN**	EMPTY **VIDE**
BUTTONED **BOUTONNÉ**	UNBUTTONED **DÉBOUTONNÉ**	NEAT **EN ORDRE**	MESSY **EN DÉSORDRE**
OPEN **OUVERT**	CLOSED **FERMÉ**	BIG **GRANDE**	SMALL **PETITE**

DIRTY
SALE

CLEAN
PROPRE

COMBED
COIFFÉ

UNCOMBED
DÉCOIFFÉ

BAREFOOT
PIEDS NUS

WITH SHOES ON
CHAUSSÉ

COMFORTABLE
CONFORTABLE

UNCOMFORTABLE
INCOMMODE

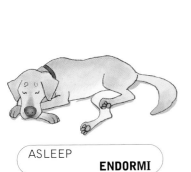

ASLEEP
ENDORMI

AWAKE
ÉVEILLÉ

UNDRESSED
DESHABILLÉ

DRESSED
HABILLÉ

DRY
SÈCHE

WET
MOUILLÉE

HAPPY
CONTENT

SAD
TRISTE

En classe

LETTERS **LES LETTRES**

SHOOTS **LES POUSSES**

PIECES OF CHALK **LES CRAIES**

STUDENTS **LES ÉLÈVES**

PHOTOGRAPH **LA PHOTO**

BACKPACK **LE SAC À DOS**

TEACHER **LE PROFESSEUR**

CLOTHES RACK **LE PORTEMANTEAU**

SHEET OF PAPER **LA FEUILLE**

WATERCOLORS **LES AQUARELLES**

PAINTS **LES POTS DE PEINTURE**

CASE **LA TROUSSE**

BLACKBOARD
LE TABLEAU

DRAWINGS
LES DESSINS

EASEL
LE CHEVALET

GIRL
LA PETITE FILLE

STEPAPER BIN
A CORBEILLE À PAPIER

BOY
LE PETIT GARÇON

JARS
LES BOÎTES

CLAY
LA PÂTE À MODELER

MAP
LA CARTE

SCISSORS
LES CISEAUX

ERASER
L'EFFACEUR

PENCIL
LE CRAYON

PENCIL SHARPENER
LE TAILLE-CRAYON

ERASER
LA GOMME

PEN
LE STYLO

MARKER
LE FEUTRE

GLUE
LA COLLE

TAPE
LE SCOTCH

BALL
LA PELOTE

PAINTBRUSH
LE PINCEAU

BINDER
LE CLASSEUR

RULER
LA RÈGLE

Colors
Les couleurs

MAROON
LE GRENAT

LIGHT BLUE
LE BLEU CLAIR

LIGHT GREEN
LE VERT CLAIR

PURPLE
LE MAUVE

BROWN
LE MARRON

RED
LE ROUGE

GRAY
LE GRIS

ORANGE
L'ORANGE

DARK GREEN
LE VERT FONCÉ

YELLOW
LE JAUNE

BLACK
LE NOIR

WHITE
LE BLANC

PINK
LE ROSE

OCHRE
L'OCRE

DARK BLUE
LE BLEU FONCÉ

Shapes
Les formes

TRIANGLE
LE TRIANGLE

CIRCLE
LE CERCLE

HALF MOON
LE CROISSANT DE LUNE

SQUARE
LE CARRÉ

RECTANGLE
LE RECTANGLE

STAR
L'ÉTOILE

HEART
LE CŒUR

OVAL
L'OVALE

L'alphabet

a b c d e f

g h i j k l

m n o p

q r s t u

v w x y z

à è ù ç œ
é
â ê î ô û
ë ï ü

Time
Le temps

MONDAY **LE LUNDI**	TUESDAY **LE MARDI**	WEDNESDAY **LE MERCREDI**	THURSDAY **LE JEUDI**

FRIDAY **LE VENDREDI**	SATURDAY **LE SAMEDI**	SUNDAY **LE DIMANCHE**

THE SEASONS
LES SAISONS DE L'ANNÉE

SPRING **LE PRINTEMPS**	SUMMER **L'ÉTÉ**	AUTUMN/FALL **L'AUTOMNE**	WINTER **L'HIVER**

THE MONTHS OF THE YEAR
LE MOIS DE L'ANNÉE

JANUARY **JANVIER**	FEBRUARY **FÉVRIER**	MARCH **MARS**	APRIL **AVRIL**	MAY **MAI**	JUNE **JUIN**

JULY **JUILLET**	AUGUST **AOÛT**	SEPTEMBER **SEPTEMBRE**	OCTOBER **OCTOBRE**	NOVEMBER **NOVEMBRE**	DECEMBER **DÉCEMBRE**

Numbers
Les números

ONE	UN
TWO	DEUX
THREE	TROIS
FOUR	QUATRE
FIVE	CINQ
SIX	SIX
SEVEN	SEPT
EIGHT	HUIT
NINE	NEUF
TEN	DIX

FIRST **LA PREMIÈRE**
SECOND **LA DEUXIÈME**
THIRD **LE TROISIÈME**
FOURTH **LE QUATRIÈME**
FIFTH **LA CINQUIÈME**
SIXTH **LA SIXIÈME**
SEVENTH **LE SEPTIÈME**
EIGHTH **LA HUITIÈME**
NINTH **LE NEUVIÈME**
TENTH **LE DIXIÈME**

BANISTER **LA RAMPE**

RAMP **LA RAMPE**

CIRCLE **LA RONDE**

BRAIDS **LES TRESSES**

PICTURES **LES IMAGES**

ALBUM **L'ALBUM**

WHISTLE **LE SIFFLET**

TOP **LA TOUPIE**

YO-YO **LE YO-YO**

MEDAL **LA MÉDAILLE**

FLOWERPOT **LE POT DE FLEURS**

WINDOW BOX **LA JARDINIÈRE**

COMIC **LA BANDE DESSINÉE**

GLASSES **LES LUNETTES**

COOKIES **LES BISCUITS**

CRUTCH **LA BÉQUILLE**

RIBBON **LE RUBAN**

HEADBAND **LE SERRE-TÊTE**

BARRETTE **L'ÉPINGLE À CHEVEUX**

BRACELET **LE BRACELET**

NECKLACE **LE COLLIER**

RING **LA BAGUE**

In the gym
Au gymnase

ROPE
LA CORDE À NŒUDS

WALL BARS
L'ESPALIER

WINDOW LADDER
L'ÉCHELLE

CRAWLING TUNNEL
LE TUNNEL

PIKE
LA PIQUE

LEOTARD
LE JUSTAUCORPS

TRACKSUIT
LE SURVÊTEMENT

KNEE PAD
LA GENOUILLIÈRE

MAT
LE TAPIS DE SOL

SWEAT
LA SUE

RIBBON
LE RUBAN

SNEAKERS
LES BASKETS

CLUB
LE MIL

36

RINGS
LES ANNEAUX

TRAMPOLINE
LE TRAMPOLINE

SPRINGBOARD
LE TREMPLIN

HOOP
LE CERCEAU

CUBE
LE CUBE

SOMERSAULT
LA PIROUETTE

WATCH
LA MONTRE

STOPWATCH
LE CHRONOMÈTRE

VAULTING BOX
LE CHEVAL DE VOLTIGE

VAULTING HORSE
LE CHEVAL D'ARÇON

PARALLEL BARS
LES BARRES PARALLÈLES

FIRE EXTINGUISHER
L'EXTINCTEUR

FLUORESCENT LIGHT
LE NÉON

Sports

Sports

GOLF • **LE GOLF**   TENNIS • **LE TENNIS**   HORSEBACK RIDING • **L'ÉQUITATION**

BASEBALL • **LE BASE-BALL**   HOCKEY • **LE HOCKEY**   RUGBY • **LE RUGBY**

SKIING • **LE SKI**   SWIMMING • **LA NATATION**   CYCLING • **LE CYCLISME**   SKATING • **LE PATINAG**

SOCCER • **LE FOOTBALL**   BASKETBALL • **LE BASKET-BALL**   HANDBALL • **LE HAND-BALL**   VOLLEYBALL • **LE VOLLEY-B**

PING-PONG • **LE PING-PONG**   MARTIAL ARTS • **LES ARTS MARTIAUX**   RACE • **LA COURSE**

HIGH JUMP •
LE SAUT EN HAUTEUR   HURDLE JUMP •
LE SAUT DES HAIES   LONG JUMP •
LE SAUT EN LONGUEUR   FENCING • **L'ESCRIME**

KING • **LA RANDONNÉE**   CLIMBING •
L'ALPINISME   CANOEING • **LE CANOË-KAYAK**   HANG GLIDING • **LE DELTAPLANE**

WBOARDING • **LE SNOWBOARD**   WINDSURFING •
LA PLANCHE À VOILE   BUNGEE JUMPING • **LE BONJI**   RAFTING • **LE RAFTING**

At the theater
Au théâtre

SPOTLIGHTS
LES PROJECTEURS
FAIRY
LA FÉE
MOON
LA LUNE
EXIT
LA SORTIE
MOUSTACHE
LA MOUSTACHE
MONSTER
LE MONSTR
GOATEE
LA BARBICHE
MUSHROOM
LE CHAMPIGNON
BEARD
LA BARBE
GHOST
LE FANTÔME
WALKING STICK
LA CANNE
USHER
L'OUVREUSE
HANDBELL
LA CLOCHETTE
DRAGON
LE DRAG
TREASURE
LE TRÉSOR
STAGE
LA SCÈNE
SPECTATORS
LES SPECTATEURS
SEATS
LES PLACES

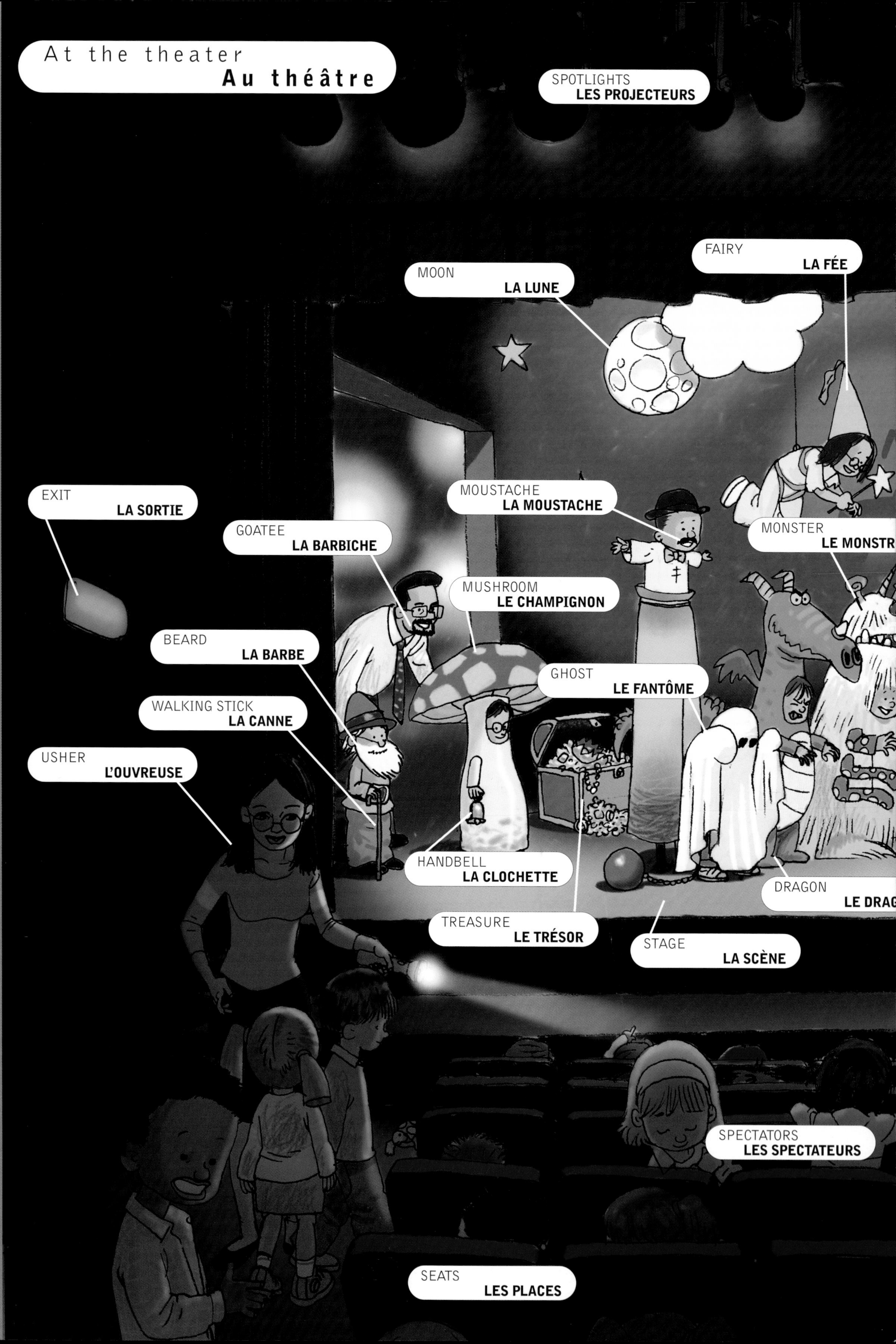

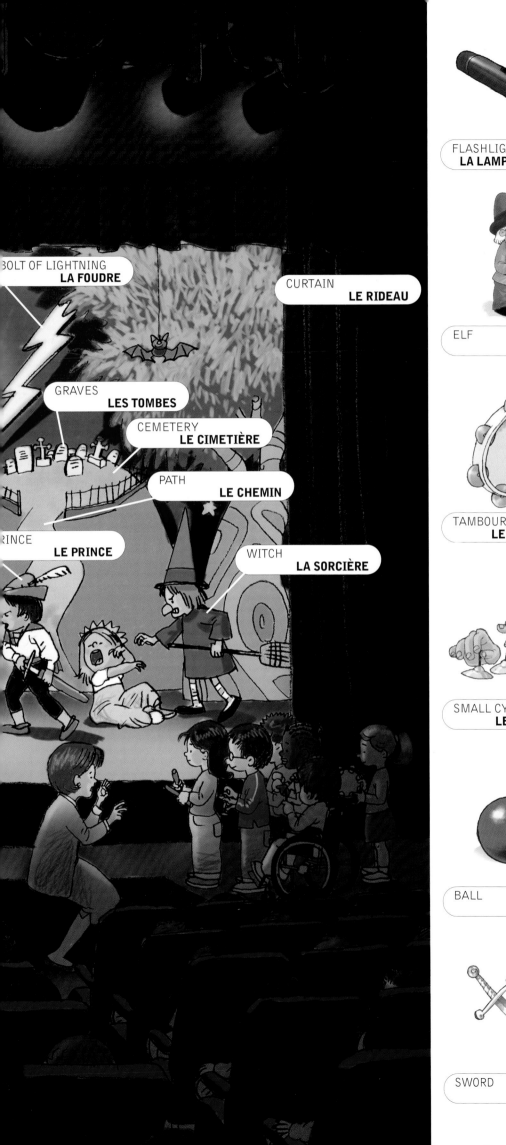

BOLT OF LIGHTNING
LA FOUDRE

CURTAIN
LE RIDEAU

GRAVES
LES TOMBES

CEMETERY
LE CIMETIÈRE

PATH
LE CHEMIN

PRINCE
LE PRINCE

WITCH
LA SORCIÈRE

FLASHLIGHT
LA LAMPE DE POCHE

WAND
LA BAGUETTE MAGIQUE

ELF
LE LUTIN

FEATHER
LA PLUME

TAMBOURINE
LE TAMBOURIN

TRIANGLE
LE TRIANGLE

SMALL CYMBALS
LES CROTALES

BAT
LA CHAUVE-SOURIS

BALL
LA BOULE

CHAIN
LA CHAÎNE

SWORD
L'ÉPÉE

BROOM
LE BALAI

Musical instruments
Instruments de musique

STRING INSTRUMENTS • INSTRUMENTS À CORDES

GUITAR • **LA GUITARE**

ELECTRIC GUITAR •
LA GUITARE ÉLECTRIQUE

BANJO • **LE BANJO**

VIOLIN • **LE VIOLON**

VIOLA • **LA VIOLE**

CELLO • **LE VIOLONCELLE**

DOUBLE BASS •
LA CONTRE-BASSE

PERCUSSION INSTRUMENTS • INSTRUMENTS À PERCUSSION

MARACAS • **LES MARACAS**

CASTANETS • **LES CASTAGNETTES**

TAMBOURINE • **LE TAMBOURIN**

DRUM • **LE TAMBOUR**

CHINESE BOX • **LA CAISSE CHINOISE**

XYLOPHONE • **LE XYLOPHONE**

CONGA DRUMS • **LES CONGAS**

KETTLE DRUM • **LA TIMBALE**

DRUM SET • **LA BATTERIE**

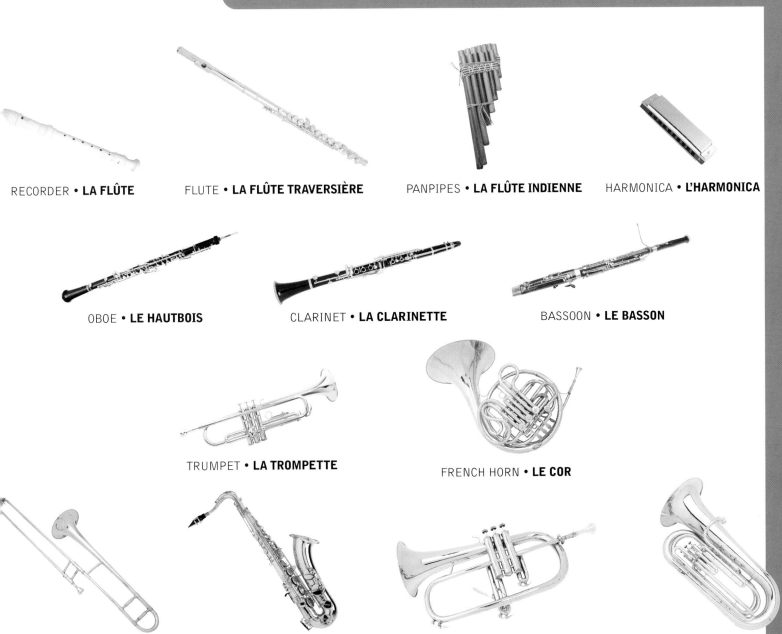

RECORDER • **LA FLÛTE**

FLUTE • **LA FLÛTE TRAVERSIÈRE**

PANPIPES • **LA FLÛTE INDIENNE**

HARMONICA • **L'HARMONICA**

OBOE • **LE HAUTBOIS**

CLARINET • **LA CLARINETTE**

BASSOON • **LE BASSON**

TRUMPET • **LA TROMPETTE**

FRENCH HORN • **LE COR**

TROMBONE • **LE TROMBONE**

SAXOPHONE • **LE SAXOPHONE**

CORNET• **LE CORNET**

TUBA • **LE TUBA**

KEYBOARD INSTRUMENTS • **INSTRUMENTS À CLAVIER**

ACCORDION • **L'ACCORDÉON**

ORGAN • **L'ORGUE**

PIANO • **LE PIANO**

On a trip to the farm
En excursion à la ferme

WINDMILL **LE MOULIN**

BARN **L'ÉTABLE**

STABLE **L'ÉCURIE**

HORSE **LE CHEVAL**

BEAM **LA POUTRE**

MARE **LA JUMENT**

PIGSTY **LA PORCHERI**

MANE **LA CRINIÈRE**

PONY **LE POULAIN**

DUCK **LE CANARD**

FARMER **LE FERMIER**

TROUGH **LA MANGEOIRE**

BUNNY **LE LAPER**

RABBIT **LE LAPIN**

PEN **LE BERCAIL**

HENS **LES POULES**

RAM **LE BÉLIER**

CHICKS **LES POUSSINS**

GOAT **LA CHÈVRE**

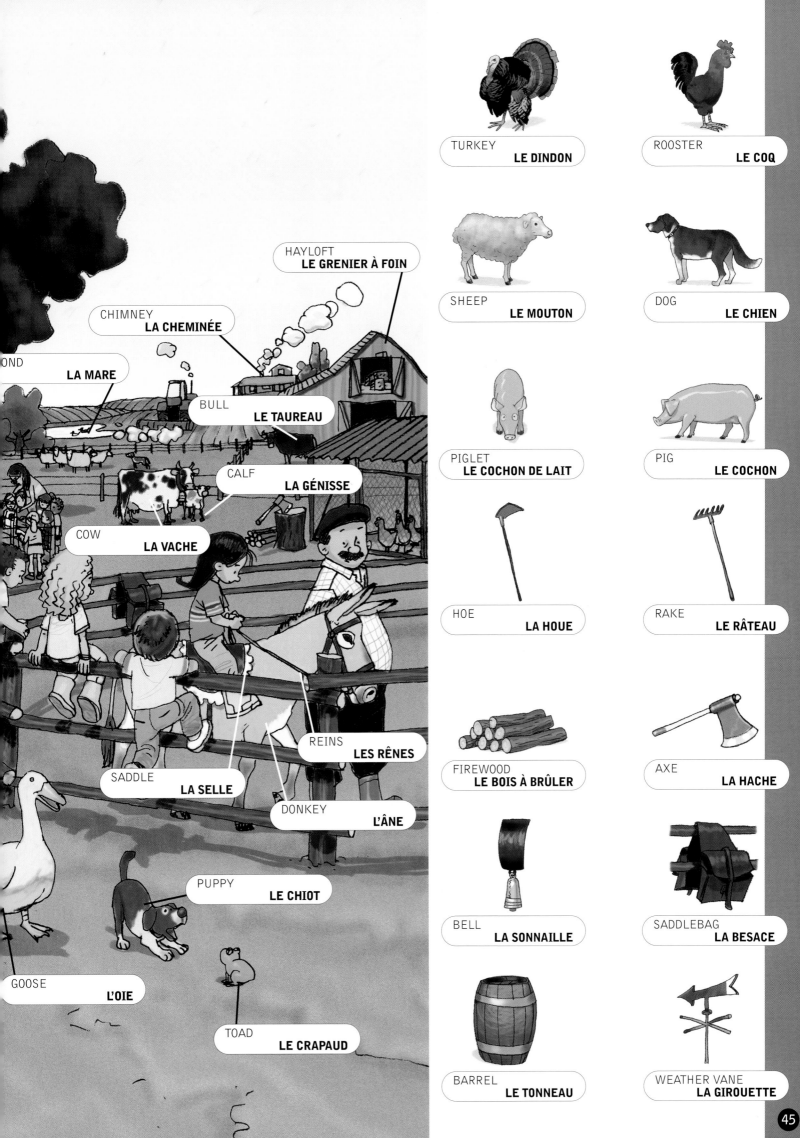

TURKEY **LE DINDON**

ROOSTER **LE COQ**

HAYLOFT **LE GRENIER À FOIN**

CHIMNEY **LA CHEMINÉE**

OND **LA MARE**

BULL **LE TAUREAU**

CALF **LA GÉNISSE**

COW **LA VACHE**

REINS **LES RÊNES**

SADDLE **LA SELLE**

DONKEY **L'ÂNE**

PUPPY **LE CHIOT**

GOOSE **L'OIE**

TOAD **LE CRAPAUD**

SHEEP **LE MOUTON**

DOG **LE CHIEN**

PIGLET **LE COCHON DE LAIT**

PIG **LE COCHON**

HOE **LA HOUE**

RAKE **LE RÂTEAU**

FIREWOOD **LE BOIS À BRÛLER**

AXE **LA HACHE**

BELL **LA SONNAILLE**

SADDLEBAG **LA BESACE**

BARREL **LE TONNEAU**

WEATHER VANE **LA GIROUETTE**

Animals
Animaux

LION • **LE LION**

TIGER • **LE TIGRE**

PANTHER • **LA PANTHÈRE**

LEOPARD • **LE LÉOPARD**

PUMA • **LE PUMA**

LYNX • **LE LYNX**

ELEPHANT • **L'ÉLÉPHANT**

HIPPOPOTAMUS • **L'HIPPOPOTAME**

RHINO • **LE RHINOCÉROS**

LLAMA • **LE LAMA**

GIRAFFE • **LA GIRAFE**

ZEBRA • **LE ZÈBRE**

BROWN BEAR • **L'OURS BRUN**   POLAR BEAR • **L'OURS POLAIRE**   PANDA BEAR • **L'OURS PANDA**

CHIMPANZEE • **LE CHIMPANZÉ**   GORILLA • **LE GORILLE**   ORANGUTAN • **L'ORANG-OUTAN**

DROMEDARY • **LE DROMADAIRE**   CAMEL • **LE CHAMEAU**   KOALA • **LE KOALA**

TORTOISE • **LA TORTUE**   SNAKE • **LE SERPENT**   KANGAROO • **LE KANGOUROU**

What are they doing?
Qu'est-ce qu'ils font?

TO READ — **LIRE**

TO SPEAK — **PARLER**

TO LISTEN — **ÉCOUTER**

TO WRITE — **ÉCRIRE**

TO COUNT — **COMPTER**

TO PLAY — **JOUER**

TO GLUE — **COLLER**

TO DRAW — **DESSINER**

TO COLOR — **COLORIER**

TO SHAPE — **MODELER**

TO ERASE — **EFFACER**

TO CROSS OUT — **RAYER**

TO CUT — **COUPER**

TO SHARPEN — **TAILLER**

TO EXPLAIN — **EXPLIQUER**

TO PLAY AN INSTRUMENT — **JOUER UN INSTRUMENT**

TO JOIN — **JOINDRE**

TO SEPARATE — **SÉPARER**

TO WRAP — **ENVELOPPER**

TO UNWRAP — **DÉBALLER**

| TO HOLD | TENIR |

| TO LET GO OF | LÂCHER |

| TO TIE UP | ATTACHER |

| TO UNTIE | DÉNOUER |

| TO BOUNCE | REBONDIR |

| TO JUMP | SAUTER |

| TO HIDE | SE CACHER |

| TO THROW | JETER |

| TO TURN SOMERSAULTS | FAIRE UNE PIROUETTE |

| TO KICK | DONNER UN COUP DE PIED |

| TO SWEAT | SUER |

| TO LIGHT | ÉCLAIRER |

| TO BUTTON | BOUTONNER |

| TO UNBUTTON | DÉBOUTONNER |

| TO PUSH | POUSSER |

| TO DRAG | TRAÎNER |

| TO SEW | COUDRE |

| TO MAKE UP | MAQUILLER |

| TO PERFORM | JOUER |

| TO GREET | SALUER |

ATTENTIVE
ATTENTIVE

DISTRACTED
DISTRAITE

UGLY
LAID

GOOD-LOOKING
BEAU

STRONG
FORT

WEAK
FAIBLE

YOUNG
JEUNE

OLD
VIEUX

TALL
GRANDE

SHORT
PETITE

FAT
GROS

THIN
MINCE

STRAIGHT
RAIDES

CURLY
FRISÉS

SHORT
COURTS

LONG
LONGS

STANDING
DEBOUT

LYING
ALLONGÉE

SEATED
ASSISE

SQUATTING
ACCROUPIE

TIRED
FATIGUÉE

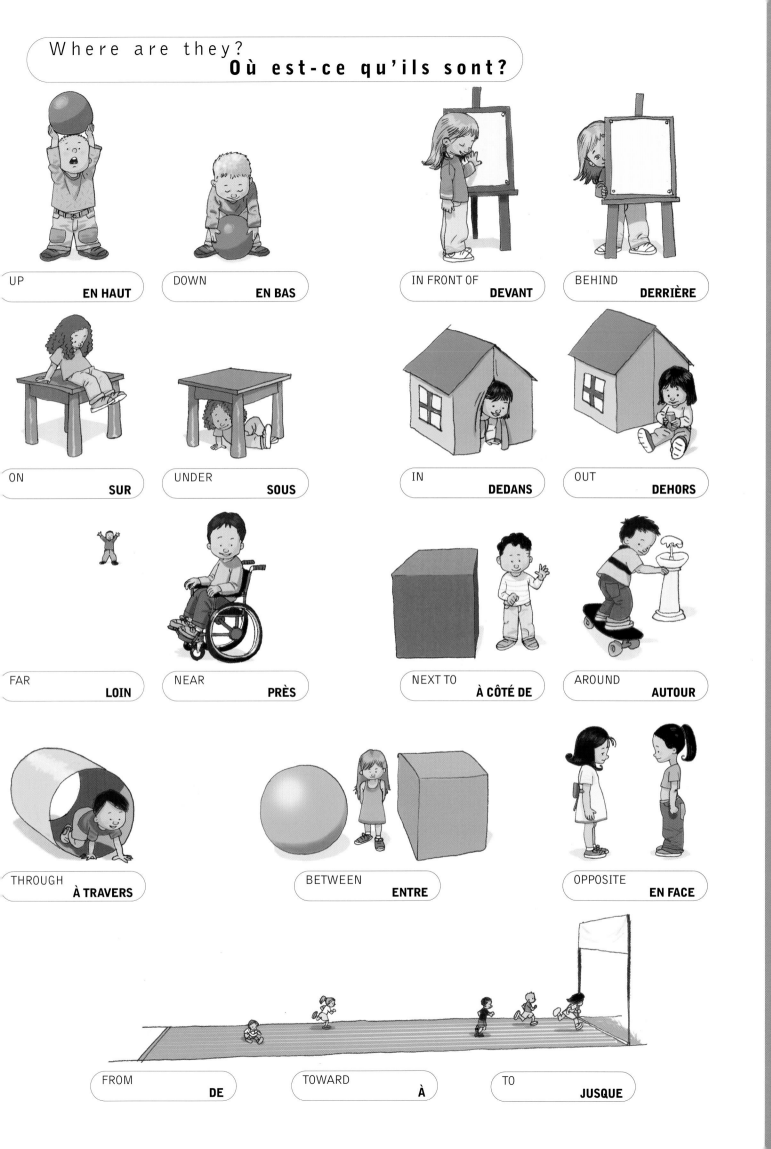

Where are they?

Où est-ce qu'ils sont?

UP **EN HAUT**

DOWN **EN BAS**

IN FRONT OF **DEVANT**

BEHIND **DERRIÈRE**

ON **SUR**

UNDER **SOUS**

IN **DEDANS**

OUT **DEHORS**

FAR **LOIN**

NEAR **PRÈS**

NEXT TO **À CÔTÉ DE**

AROUND **AUTOUR**

THROUGH **À TRAVERS**

BETWEEN **ENTRE**

OPPOSITE **EN FACE**

FROM **DE**

TOWARD **À**

TO **JUSQUE**

BALCONIES **LES BALCON**

MOVIE THEATER **LE CINÉMA**

CHURCH **L'ÉGLISE**

POST OFFICE **LA POSTE**

HOTEL **L'HÔTEL**

STORE **LE MAGASIN**

BREAKDOWN **LA PANNE**

DRAIN **LE CANIVEAU**

SLIDE **LE TOBOGGAN**

BENCH **LE BANC**

PARK **LE PARC**

BUS STOP **L'ARRÊT DE BUS**

MEMORIAL **LE MONUMENT**

PIGEONS **LES PIGEONS**

CRUMBS **LES MIETTES**

PUDDLE **LA FLAQUE**

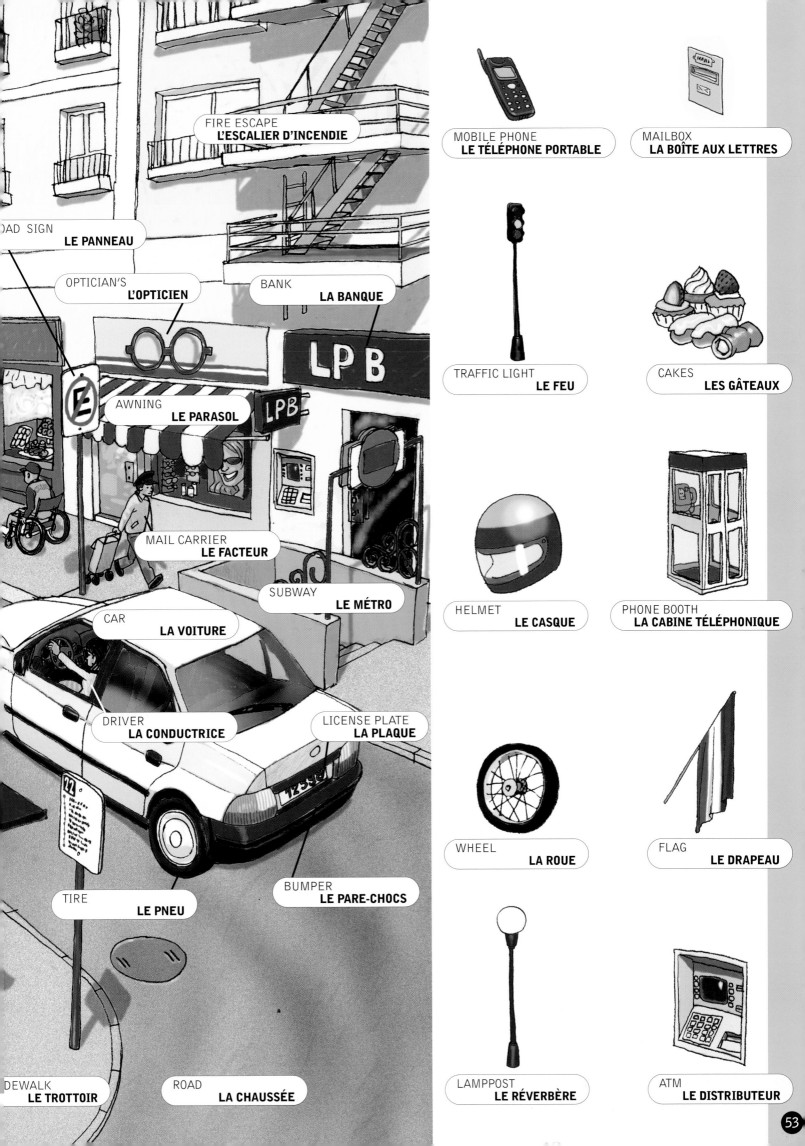

FIRE ESCAPE
L'ESCALIER D'INCENDIE

OAD SIGN
LE PANNEAU

OPTICIAN'S
L'OPTICIEN

BANK
LA BANQUE

AWNING
LE PARASOL

MAIL CARRIER
LE FACTEUR

SUBWAY
LE MÉTRO

CAR
LA VOITURE

DRIVER
LA CONDUCTRICE

LICENSE PLATE
LA PLAQUE

BUMPER
LE PARE-CHOCS

TIRE
LE PNEU

DEWALK
LE TROTTOIR

ROAD
LA CHAUSSÉE

MOBILE PHONE
LE TÉLÉPHONE PORTABLE

MAILBOX
LA BOÎTE AUX LETTRES

TRAFFIC LIGHT
LE FEU

CAKES
LES GÂTEAUX

HELMET
LE CASQUE

PHONE BOOTH
LA CABINE TÉLÉPHONIQUE

WHEEL
LA ROUE

FLAG
LE DRAPEAU

LAMPPOST
LE RÉVERBÈRE

ATM
LE DISTRIBUTEUR

53

BICYCLE • **LA BICYCLETTE**

SKATES • **LES PATINS**

SCOOTER • **LA PATINETTE**

SKATEBOARD •
LA PLANCHE À ROULETTES

TRICYCLE • **LE TRICYCLE**

WALKIE-TALKIE • **LE TALKIE-WALKIE**

LEGO BRICKS • **LES BRIQUES EN PLASTIQUE**

TEDDY BEAR • **LA PELUCHE**

JIGSAW PUZZLE • **LE PUZZLE**

PUZZLE • **LE CASSE-TÊTE**

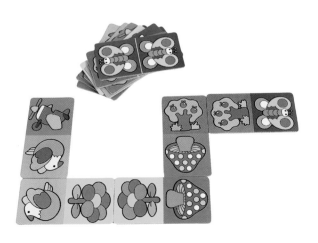

DOMINOES • **LES DOMINOS**

54

VIDEO GAME • **LE JEU VIDÉO**

DOLL • **LA POUPÉE**

CAR • **LA VOITURE**

CHESS • **LES ÉCHECS**

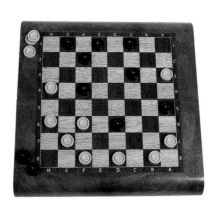

CHECKERS • **LES DAMES**

PARCHEESI • **LE JEU DES PETITS CHEVAUX**

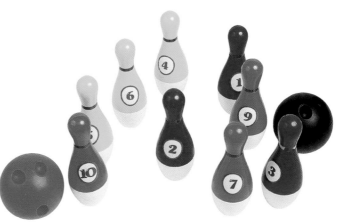

BOWLING • **LES QUILLES**

PUPPETS • **LES MARIONNETTES**

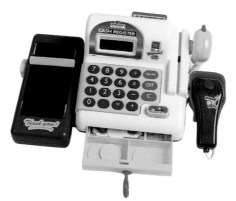

CASH REGISTER •
LA CAISSE ENREGISTREUSE

ROCKING HORSE •
LE PETIT CHEVAL DE BOIS

At the supermarket
Au supermarché

FRUIT STALL
LE MARCHAND DE FRUITS

FISHMONGER
LA POISSONIÈRE

BUTCHER'S
LA BOUCHERIE

BUTCHER
LE BOUCHER

APRON
LE TABLIER

COUNTER
LE COMPTOIR

MEAT
LA VIANDE

FISH
LE POISSON

FRUIT
LES FRUITS

56

CANNED FOOD
LES CONSERVES

BANNER
LE FANION

CASHIER
LA CAISSIÈRE

CONTAINER
LE CONTENEUR

STROLLER
LA POUSSETTE

SHOPPING CART
LE CADDIE

FROZEN FOOD
LES SURGELÉS

COIN PURSE
LE PORTE-MONNAIE

COINS
LES PIÈCES

WALLET
LE PORTEFEUILLE

PURSE
LE SAC

MITTENS
LES MOUFLES

GLOVES
LES GANTS

HAT
LE BONNET

SCARF
LE FOULARD

SCARF
L'ÉCHARPE

BAR CODE
LE CODE À BARRES

BASKET
LE PANIER

SCALES
LA BALANCE

SKULL **LE CRÂNE**

MUSCLES **LES MUSCLES**

X-RAY **LA RADIOGRAPHIE**

LUNG **LE POUMON**

HEART **LE CŒUR**

NURSE **L'INFIRMIÈRE**

MEDICINE **LES MÉDICAMENTS**

STOMACH **L'ESTOMAC**

STRETCHER **LE BRANCARD**

INJURY **LA BLESSURE**

DOCTOR **LE MÉDECIN**

BAND-AID **LE PANSEMENT**

PATIENT **LE PATIENT**

MEDICAL TAPE **LE SPARADRAP**

GAUZE BANDAGE **LA GAZE**

ALCOHOL **L'ALCOOL**

MASK **LE MASQUE**

OFFICE **LE CABINET**

BATHROOMS
LES TOILETTES

SIGN
L'AFFICHE

CAST
LE PLÂTRE

SEAT
LE SIÈGE

WAITING ROOM
LA SALLE D'ATTENTE

BANDAGE
LA BANDE

COTTON
LE COTON

SYRINGE
LA SERINGUE

THERMOMETER
LE THERMOMÈTRE

STETHOSCOPE
LE STÉTHOSCOPE

SYRUP
LE SIROP

PILLS
LES CACHETS

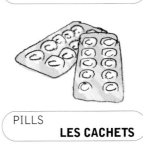

OINTMENT
LA POMMADE

INFORMATION BOARD
LE PANNEAU D'AFFICHAGE

LOUD SPEAKERS
LES HAUT-PARLEURS

INFORMATION DESK
L'INFORMATION

ENGINE DRIVER
LE MÉCANICIEN

CLEANER
LA FEMME DE NETTOYAGE

CAMERA
L'APPAREIL PHOTO

SUITCASE
LA VALISE

TOURIST
LE TOURISTE

COLLECTOR
LE CONTRÔLEUR

CLEANER'S CART
LE CHARIOT DE NETTOYAGE

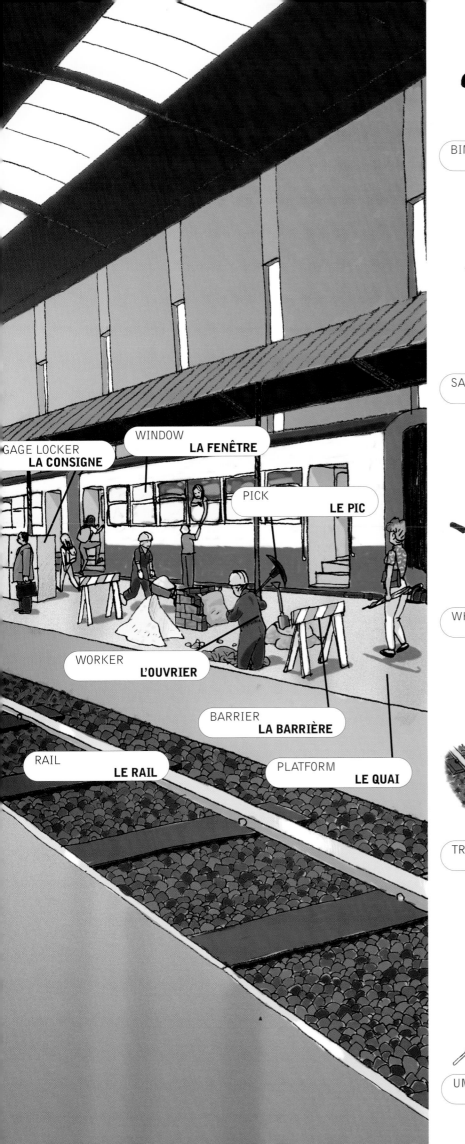

GAGE LOCKER **LA CONSIGNE**

WINDOW **LA FENÊTRE**

PICK **LE PIC**

WORKER **L'OUVRIER**

BARRIER **LA BARRIÈRE**

RAIL **LE RAIL**

PLATFORM **LE QUAI**

BINOCULARS **LES JUMELLES**

PASSENGER CAR **LE WAGON DE PASSAGERS**

SACK **LE SAC**

FREIGHT CAR **LE FOURGON**

WHEELBARROW **LA BROUETTE**

CAMCORDER **LE CAMÉSCOPE**

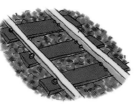
TRACK **LA VOIE**

NEWSPAPER **LE JOURNAL**

UMBRELLA **LE PARAPLUIE**

CART **LE CHARIOT**

Moyens de transport

BY LAND • PAR TERRE

CAR • **LA VOITURE** RACE CAR • **LA VOITURE DE COURSE** VAN • **LA FOURGONNETTE**

AMBULANCE • **L'AMBULANCE** FIRE ENGINE • **LA VOITURE DE POMPIERS** MOTORCYCLE • **LA MOTO**

BUS • **L'AUTOBUS** TAXI • **LE TAXI** TRAIN • **LE TRAIN**

TRUCK • **LE CAMION** TRACTOR • **LE TRACTEUR** EXCAVATOR • **L'EXCAVATRICE**

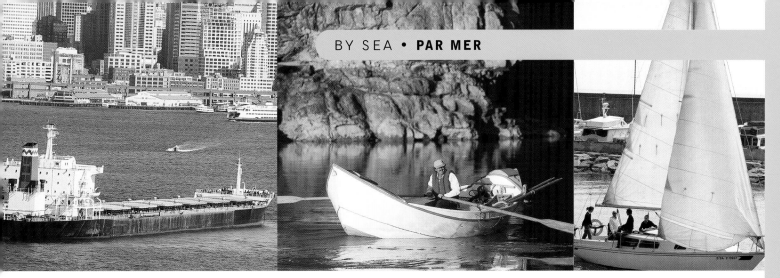

SHIP • **LE BATEAU**   ROWBOAT • **LE BATEAU À RAMES**   SAILBOAT • **LE VOILIER**

SPEEDBOAT • **LA VEDETTE**   CANOE • **LE CANOË**   YACHT • **LE YACHT**

BY AIR • **PAR L'AIR**

PLANE • **L'AVION**   ROCKET • **LA FUSÉE**   LIGHT AIRCRAFT • **LE PETIT AVION**

ULTRALIGHT • **L'U.L.M.**   HOT-AIR BALLOON • **LE BALLON**   HELICOPTER • **L'HÉLICOPTÈRE**

TO STROLL
SE PROMENER

TO GO UP
MONTER

TO GO DOWN
DESCENDRE

TO WAIT
ATTENDRE

TO GO IN
ENTRER

TO GO OUT
SORTIR

TO OPEN
OUVRIR

TO CLOSE
FERMER

TO CROSS
TRAVERSER

TO SLIP
GLISSER

TO STUMBLE
TRÉBUCHER

TO TALK ON THE PHONE
PARLER AU TÉLÉPHONE

TO RIDE A BICYCLE
FAIRE DE LA BICYCLETTE

TO TAKE OFF
DÉCOLLER

TO LAND
ATTERRIR

TO DRIVE
CONDUIRE

64

TO BREATHE
RESPIRER

TO BLOW ONE'S NOSE
SE MOUCHER

TO CURE
GUÉRIR

TO BANDAGE
BANDER

TO LAUGH
RIRE

TO CRY
PLEURER

TO SNEEZE
ÉTERNUER

TO COUGH
TOUSSER

TO GUARD
GARDER

TO LOAD
CHARGER

TO UNLOAD
DÉCHARGER

TO WEIGH
PESER

TO SPEED UP
ACCÉLÉRER

TO PASS
DÉPASSER

TO TURN
VIRER

TO BRAKE
FREINER

TO CRASH
ENTRER EN COLLISION

TO TRAVEL
VOYAGER

TO SAY GOOD-BYE
DIRE AU REVOIR

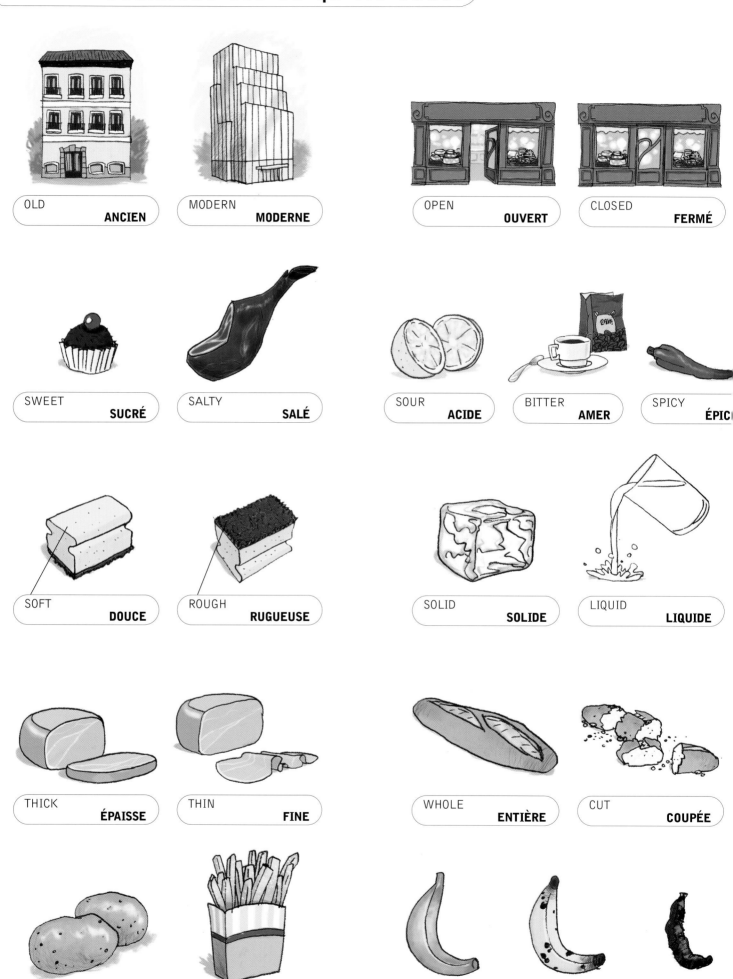

OLD **ANCIEN**

MODERN **MODERNE**

OPEN **OUVERT**

CLOSED **FERMÉ**

SWEET **SUCRÉ**

SALTY **SALÉ**

SOUR **ACIDE**

BITTER **AMER**

SPICY **ÉPIC**

SOFT **DOUCE**

ROUGH **RUGUEUSE**

SOLID **SOLIDE**

LIQUID **LIQUIDE**

THICK **ÉPAISSE**

THIN **FINE**

WHOLE **ENTIÈRE**

CUT **COUPÉE**

RAW **CRUES**

FRIED **FRITES**

UNRIPE **VERTE**

RIPE **MÛRE**

SPOILED **GÂTÉ**

HARD **DUR**

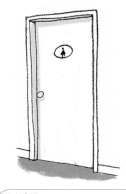

SOFT **MOU**

WITH THE LID ON **FERMÉE**

WITH THE LID OFF **SANS COUVERCLE**

FREE **LIBRE**

BUSY **OCUPÉE**

NERVOUS **NERVEUSE**

CALM **TRANQUILLE**

HEALTHY **SAIN**

SICK **MALADE**

INDUSTRIOUS **TRAVAILLEUR**

LAZY **PARESSEUX**

BORED **ENNUYÉE**

WITH A COLD **ENRHUMÉ**

GREEDY **GOURMANDE**

CURIOUS **CURIEUX**

RAINBOW
L'ARC-EN-CIEL

ISLAND
L'ÎLE

LIGHTHOUSE
LE PHARE

PEDAL BOAT
LE PÉDALO

BOAT
LA BARQUE

SEA
LA MER

WAVE
LA VAGUE

SAND
LE SABLE

SUNSCREEN
LA CRÈME SOLAIRE

SHELL **LA COQUILLE**

CRAB **LE CRABE**

BUCKET **LE SEAU**

SHOVEL **LA PELLE**

MOLD **LE MOULE**

WATERING CAN **L'ARROSOIR**

SUNGLASSES **LES LUNETTES DE SOLEIL**

ICE-CREAM CONE **LE CORNET**

ICE-CREAM POP **LA GLACE À L'EAU**

INNER TUBE **LA BOUÉE**

FLOATS **LES FLOTTEURS**

LIFE JACKET **LE GILET DE SAUVETAGE**

CAP **LA CASQUETTE**

GOGGLES **LES LUNETTES DE PLONGÉE**

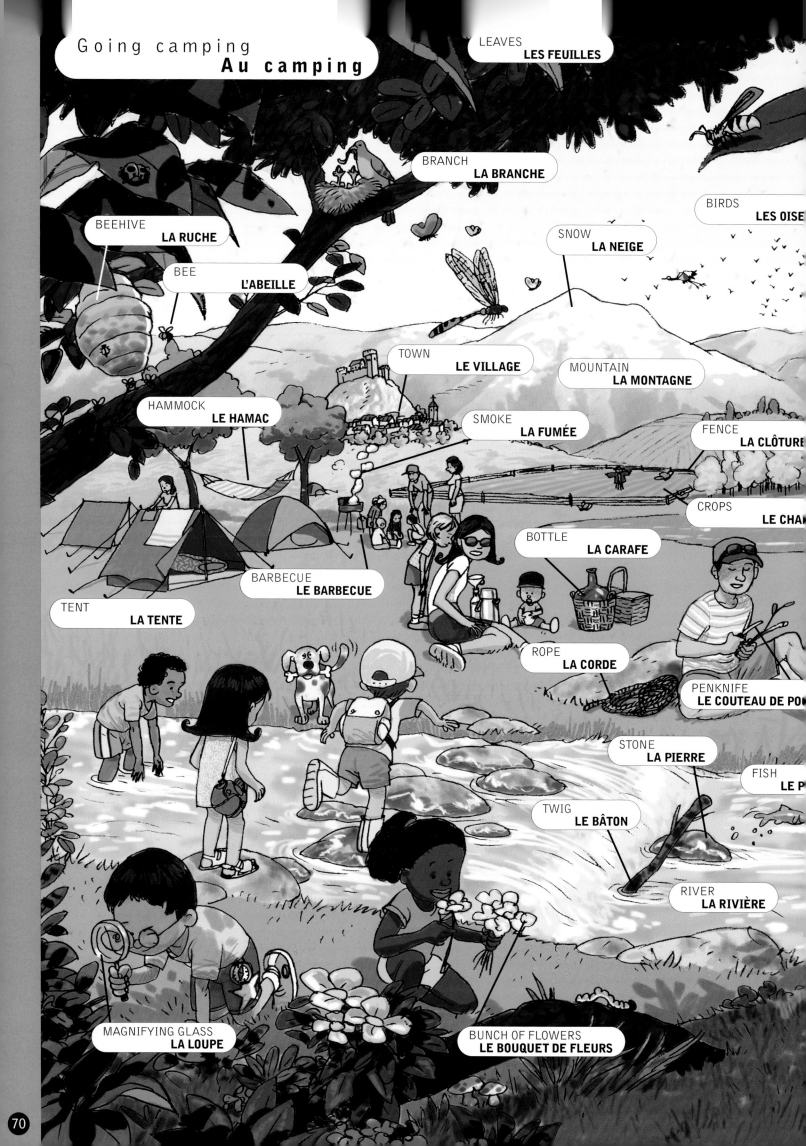

LEAVES **LES FEUILLES**

BRANCH **LA BRANCHE**

BIRDS **LES OISE**

BEEHIVE **LA RUCHE**

SNOW **LA NEIGE**

BEE **L'ABEILLE**

TOWN **LE VILLAGE**

MOUNTAIN **LA MONTAGNE**

HAMMOCK **LE HAMAC**

SMOKE **LA FUMÉE**

FENCE **LA CLÔTURE**

CROPS **LE CHA**

BOTTLE **LA CARAFE**

BARBECUE **LE BARBECUE**

TENT **LA TENTE**

ROPE **LA CORDE**

PENKNIFE **LE COUTEAU DE PO**

STONE **LA PIERRE**

FISH **LE P**

TWIG **LE BÂTON**

RIVER **LA RIVIÈRE**

MAGNIFYING GLASS **LA LOUPE**

BUNCH OF FLOWERS **LE BOUQUET DE FLEURS**

SPIDER'S WEB
LA TOILE D'ARAIGNÉE

SPIDER
L'ARAIGNÉE

FOREST
LE BOIS

FISHING ROD
LA CANNE À PÊCHE

FISHERMAN
LE PÊCHEUR

LAKE
LE LAC

SHEPHERD
LE BERGER

FLOCK OF SHEEP
LE TROUPEAU

ANTS
LES FOURMIS

GRASS
L'HERBE

DRAGONFLY
LA LIBELLULE

BONE
L'OS

SNAIL
L'ESCARGOT

BUTTERFLY
LE PAPILLON

THERMOS
LE THERMOS

COMPASS
LA BOUSSOLE

NEST
LE NID

LADYBUG
LA COCCINELLE

LIZARD
LE LÉZARD

WATER BOTTLE
LA GOURDE

CATERPILLAR
LE CHENILLE

SCARECROW
L'ÉPOUVANTAIL

At the fair
À la fête

PAPER LANTERN
LE LAMPION

ROLLER COASTER
LES MONTAGNES RUSSES

FERRIS WHEEL
LA GRANDE ROUE

INFLATABLE CASTLE
LE CHÂTEAU GONFLABLE

MERRY-GO-ROUND
LE MANÈGE

CART
LA CHARRETTE

SINGER
LE CHANTEUR

MAGICIAN
LE MAGICIEN

SKELETON
LE SQUELETTE

JUGGLER
LE JONGLEUR

WIG
LA PERRUQUE

CLOWN
LE CLOWN

CAT
LE CHAT

FORTUNE-TELLER
LA DEVINERESSE

BELL
LE GRELOT

CRYSTAL BALL
LA BOULE DE VERRE

CANDLESTICKS
LES BOURGEOIRS

MASK
LE MASQUE

SPACESHIP
LE VAISSEAU SPATIAL

PUPPET
LA MARIONNETTE

URGICAL COLLAR
LA MINERVE

BUBBLE
LA BOULE

TARGET SHOOTING
LE TIR À LA CIBLE

SOFT DRINK
LE RAFRAÎCHISSEMENT

BULL'S-EYE
LA CIBLE

DART
LE DARD

TURBAN
LE TURBAN

TOP HAT
LE HAUT-DE-FORME

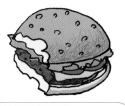

HAMBURGER
LE HAMBURGER

CANDY CANE
LE BÂTON À BONBON

COUPLE
LE COUPLE

HOT DOG
LE HOT-DOG

MICROPHONE
LE MICRO

POTATO CHIPS
LES CHIPS

POPCORN
LE POP-CORN

COTTON CANDY
LA BARBE À PAPA

RACE DRIVER
LE PILOTE

FIREMAN
LE POMPIER

PHOTOGRAPHER
LA PHOTOGRAPHE

PAINTER
LE PEINTRE

POLICEWOMAN
LA FEMME POLICIER

BALLET DANCER
LA DANSEUSE

MECHANIC
LA MÉCANICIENNE

COWGIRL
LA COW-GIRL

COWBOY
LE COW-BOY

COOK
LA CUISINIÈRE

SCIENTIST
LE SCIENTIFIQUE

ASTRONAUT
L'ASTRONAUTE

KNIGHT
LE CHEVALIER

CAVEWOMAN
LA FEMME PRÉHISTORIQUE

SULTAN
LE SULTAN

JESTER
LE BOUFFON

PIRATE
LE PIRATE

KING
LE ROI

SOLDIER
LE SOLDAT

SUPERHERO
LE SUPERHÉROS

MOUSE
LA SOURIS

MUSKETEER
LE MOUSQUETAIRE

ANGEL
L'ANGE

DEVIL
LE DIABLE

TO PUT CREAM ON
SE METTRE DE LA CRÈME

TO SUNBATHE
PRENDRE LE SOLEIL

TO SHIVER
GRELOTTER

TO MELT
FONDRE

TO BUILD
CONSTRUIRE

TO WATER
ARROSER

TO TAKE A SHOWER
SE DOUCHER

TO SPLASH
ÉCLABOUSSER

TO FLOAT
FLOTTER

TO SINK
COULER

TO DIVE
FAIRE DE LA PLONGÉE

TO WATCH
OBSERVER

TO CAMP
CAMPER

TO POINT
MONTRER

TO SAIL
NAVIGUER

TO ROW
RAMER

TO WALK
MARCHER

TO RUN
COURIR

TO FLY
VOLER

TO SLITHER
RAMPER

TO SUCKLE **TÉTER**

TO LICK **LÉCHER**

TO LICK **SUCER**

TO SCRATCH **GRIFFER**

TO STING **PIQUER**

TO ATTACK **ATTAQUER**

TO SNIFF **FLAIRER**

TO CLIMB **ESCALADER**

TO FISH **PÊCHER**

TO PAINT **PEINDRE**

TO NAIL **CLOUER**

TO MOW **MOISSONNER**

TO PRUNE **TAILLER**

TO SAW **SCIER**

TO DIG **CREUSER**

TO PLOW **LABOURER**

TO BREAK UP **PIQUER**

TO CHOP DOWN **ABATTRE**

TO SOW **SEMER**

What are they like?
Comment est-ce qu'ils sont?

SUNNY **ENSOLEILLÉ**   CLOUDY **NUAGEUX**

NARROW **ÉTROIT**   WIDE **LARGE**

FAST **RAPIDE**   SLOW **LENTE**

CAUGHT **PRISONNIÈRE**   FREE **LIBRE**

DIFFICULT **DIFFICILE**   EASY **FACILE**

RESISTANT **RÉSISTANTE**   FRAGILE **FRAGILE**

INFLATED **GONFLÉE**   DEFLATED **DÉGONFLÉE**

FOLDED **PLIÉ**   STRETCHED **ÉTIRÉ**

ALIKE **PAREILLES**

DIFFERENT **DIFFÉRENTS**

PALE **PÂLE**

TANNED **BRONZÉE**

STRANGE **ÉTRANGE**

NORMAL **NORMALE**

COWARDLY **LÂCHE**

BRAVE **COURAGEUX**

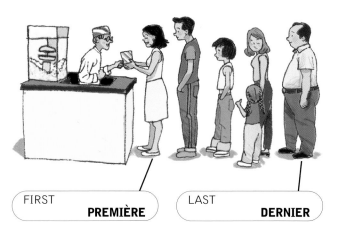

FIRST **PREMIÈRE**

LAST **DERNIER**

WELL-MANNERED **BIEN ÉLEVÉE**

BAD-MANNERED **MAL ÉLEVÉE**

DOMESTIC **DOMESTIQUE**

WILD **SAUVAGE**

TAME **TRANQUILLE**

FIERCE **FÉROCE**

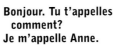

Good morning. What's your name?
My name is Anne.

Bonjour. Tu t'appelles comment?
Je m'appelle Anne.

Good afternoon. How are you?
I'm very good, thank you.

Bonjour. Comment ça va?

Très bien, merci.

How old is the baby?
He's one. Happy birthday!

Le bébé a quel âge?
Il a un an. Bon anniversaire!

What is today's date?

Today is Sunday, the 4th of July.

Nous sommes quel jour aujourd'hui?
Nous sommes dimanche, le quatre juillet, aujourd'hui.

I'm cold!

J'ai froid!

I'm sick.

Je suis malade.

Helen is thirsty.

Hélène a soif.

I'm scared.

J'ai peur.

Are you hot?
No, I'm tired.

As-tu chaud?
Non, je suis fatigué.

How is Christine?
She's sad.

Comment est Christine?
Elle est triste.

The sisters are happy.
The friends are happy, too.

Les sœurs sont contentes.
Les amis sont contents aussi.

It's sunny.

Il fait du soleil.

It's raining. See you later!

Il pleut. À bientôt!

What are you wearing?
I'm wearing shoes.

Qu'est-ce que tu portes?
Je porte les chaussures.

What color is your skirt?
My skirt is purple.

De quelle couleur est ta jupe?
Ma jupe est mauve.

What is Mary doing?
She's jumping rope.

Qu'est-ce que Marie fait?
Elle saute à la corde.

What are you doing, George?

I'm throwing the ball.

Qu'est-ce que tu fais, Georges?
Je lance le ballon.

What is Robert doing?
He's eating because he is hungry.

Qu'est-ce que Robert fait?
Il mange parce qu'il a faim.

Who is kissing the boy?
The girl is kissing the boy.

Qui embrasse le garçon?
La fille embrasse le garçon.

Who is holding the book?
The teacher is holding the book.

Qui tient le livre?
Le profeseur tient le livre.

Where are you?
I'm inside the house.

Où es-tu?
Je suis dans la maison.

Look right. Look left.

Now cross the street.

Regarde à droite. Regarde à gauche.
Maintenant traverse la rue.

Here comes the bus. Where are you going?
I'm going to school.

L'autobus vient. Où est-ce que tu vas?
Je vais à l'école.

What are you going to do?
I'm going to play soccer.

Qu'est-ce que tu vas faire?
Je vais jouer au football.

FRENCH-ENGLISH GLOSSARY AND PRONUNCIATION

Look at the pronunciation guide in parentheses after each French word or expression in this word list. It will teach you to pronounce the French words and phrases as the French do. When you pronounce the guides out loud, read them as you would read words and syllables in English.

Notice that French has some sounds that are not found in English. Here are the symbols we use to show these sounds. Some of them are shown as capital letters, which will help you spot them easily.

R   The French **r** (as in **bonjour**, **Robert**) is pronounced at the back of the throat, a bit like gargling.

uh   The letter combinations **eu**, **œu** (as in **peu**, **œufs**), and sometimes the letters **e** (as in **de**, **je**, **que**) and **o** (as in **port**, **accord**, **sorbet**), are spelled **uh** in the guides. To say this sound, hold your tongue as if to make the "ay" sound and round your lips as if to make the "o" sound.

ERR   This sound is a more "open" version of the one above (**uh**). It is usually found in the letter combinations **-eur** or **-œur** (as in **chanteur**, **leur**, **sœur**).

U   To pronounce the French **u** (usually a single **u** in spelling, as in **tu**, **rue**, **jupe**), hold your tongue as if to make the "ee" sound and round your lips as if to make the "o" sound.

A^n, I^n, O^n   French also has several sounds called "nasalized" vowels, spelled with the letters **a**, **e**, **i**, **o** immediately preceding the letter **n** (as in **manteau**, **main**, **mon**). Pronounce these vowels through your mouth and nose at the same time. They are shown in the guides with the symbols at the left.

Hints: When you read the pronunciation guides aloud, always pronounce a single "e" like the "e" in the English word "let." The letter (sound) **a** has been written **ah**; in French, the letter **a** always sounds like the "a" in "father." All French words give a slight emphasis to their final syllable.

à (ah) toward 51
à côté de (ah-ko-tay) next to 51
à travers (ah-tRah-veR) through 51
abattre (ah-bah-tR) to chop down 77
l'abeille (f.) (lah-bay) bee 70
l'abricot (m.) (lah-bRee-ko) apricot 11
accélérer (ahk-say-lay-Ray) to speed up 65
l'accordéon (m.) (lah-kuhR-day-O^n) accordion 43
accroupie (ah-kRoo-pee) squatting 50
acide (ah-seed) sour 66
l'affiche (f.) (lah-feesh) sign 59
l'ail (m.) (lai) garlic 10
l'aimant (m.) (lay-mA^n) magnet 9
l'air (m.) (leR) air 63
l'album (m.) (lahl-buhm) album 35
l'alcool (m.) (ahl-kuhl) alcohol 58
allongée (ah-lO^n-jay) lying (down) 50
allumée (ah-lU-may) on 26
les allumettes (f.) (lay-zah-lU-met) matches 7
l'alphabet (m.) (lahl-fah-bay) alphabet 31
l'alpinisme (m.) (lahl-pee-nees-muh) climbing 39
les amandes (f.) (lay-zah-mA^nd) almonds 10
l'ambulance (f.) (lA^n-bU-lA^ns) ambulance 62
amer (ah-meR) bitter 66
les anacardes (m.) (lay-zah-nah-kahRd) cashew nuts 10
l'ananas (m.) (lah-nah-nah) pineapple 11
ancien (A^n-syI^n) old 66
l'âne (m.) (lahn) donkey 45
l'ange (m.) (lA^nj) angel 75
les animaux (m.) (lay-zah-nee-mo) animals 46
les anneaux (m.) (lay-zah-no) rings 37
l'année (f.) (lah-nay) year 32
l'annulaire (m.) (lah-nU-leR) ring finger 19
août (oot) August 32
l'appareil photo (m.) (lah-pah-Ray-fo-to) camera 60

les aquarelles (f.) (lay-zah-kwah-Rel) watercolors 28
l'araignée (f.) (lah-Ray-nyay) spider 71
l'arbre (m.) (lahR-bR) tree 71
l'arc-en-ciel (m.) (lahRk-A^n-syel) rainbow 69
l'armoire (f.) (lahR-mwahR) armoire 15
l'arrêt de bus (m.) (lah-Ray-duh-bUs) bus stop 52
arroser (ah-Ro-zay) to water 76
l'arrosoir (m.) (lah-Ro-zwahR) watering can 69
l'artichaut (m.) (lahR-tee-sho) artichoke 10
les arts martiaux (m.) (lay-zahR-mahR-syo) martial arts 39
les asperges (f.) (lay-zah-speRj) white asparagus 10
les asperges vertes (f.) (lay-zah-speRj-veRt) green asparagus 10
l'aspirateur (m.) (lah-spee-Rah-tERR) vacuum cleaner 12
l'assiette (f.) (lah-syet) plate 9
assise (ah-seez) seated 50
l'astronaute (m./f.). (lah-stRo-not) astronaut 74
attacher (ah-tah-shay) to tie up 49
attaquer (ah-tah-kay) to attack 77
attendre (ah-tA^ndR) to wait 64
attentive (ah-tA^n-teev) attentive 50
atterrir (ah-tay-ReeR) to land 64
l'autobus (m.) (luh-tuh-bUs) bus 62
l'automne (m.) (luh-tuhn) autumn/fall 32
autour (o-tooR) around 51
l'avant-bras (m.) (lah-vA^n-bRah) forearm 19
l'avion (m.) (lah-vyO^n) plane 63
l'avocat (m.) (lah-vo-kah) avocado 11
avril (ah-vReel) April 32

la bague (lah-bahg) ring 35
la baguette magique (lah-bah-get-mah-jeek) magic wand 41

la baignoire (lah-be-nywahR) bath 16
bâiller (bai-yay) to yawn 25
le balai (luh-bah-lay) broom 41
la balance (lah-bah-lA^ns) scale 16; scales 57
balayer (bah-lay-yay) to sweep 25
les balcons (m.) (lay-bahl-kO^n) balconies 52
le ballon (luh-bah-lO^n) ball 21, 34; hot-air balloon 63
les ballons (m.) (lay-bah-lO^n) balloons 6
la banane (lah-bah-nahn) banana 11
le banc (luh-bA^n) bench 52
la bande (lah-bA^nd) bandage 59
la bande dessinée (lah-bA^nd-day-see-nay) comic (strip) 35
bander (bA^n-day) to bandage 65
le banjo (luh-bA^n-jo) banjo 42
la banque (lah-bA^nk) bank 53
la barbe (lah-bahRb) beard 40
la barbe à papa (lah-bahR-bah-pah-pah) cotton candy 73
le barbecue (luh-bahR-buh-kyU) barbecue 70
la barbiche (lah-bahR-beesh) goatee 40
la barque (lah-bahRk) boat 69
la barre (lah-bahR) bar 9
les barres parallèles (f.) (lay-bahR-pah-Rah-lel) parallel bars 37
la barrière (lah-bah-RyeR) barrier 61
le base-ball (luh-bayz-bol) baseball 38
le basket-ball (luh-bahs-ket-bol) basketball 38
les baskets (m.) (lay-bahs-ket) sneakers 23, 36
le basson (luh-bah-sO^n) bassoon 43
le bateau (luh-bah-to) ship 63
le bateau à rames (luh-bah-to-ah-Rahm) rowboat 63
le bâton (luh-bah-tO^n) twig 70
le bâton à bonbon (luh-bah-tO^n-ah-bO^n-bO^n) candy cane 73
la batterie (lah-bah-tRee) drum set 42
battre (bahtR) to whisk 24

le **bavoir** (luh-bah-vwahR) bib 8

beau (bo) good-looking 50

le **bébé** (luh-bay-bay) baby 6

le **bélier** (luh-bay-lyay) ram 44

la **béquille** (lah-bay-kee) crutch 35

le **bercail** (luh-beR-kai) pen 44

le **berceau** (luh-beR-so) crib 15, 20

le **berger** (luh-beR-jay) shepherd 71

la **besace** (lah-buh-sahs) saddlebag 45

le **biberon** (luh-bee-bRO^n) baby's bottle 21

la **bibliothèque** (lah-bee-blee-yo-tek) bookcase 15

la **bicyclette** (lah-bee-see-klet) bicycle 54

le **bidet** (luh-bee-day) bidet 16

bien élévée (byeh-nay-luh-vay) well-mannered 79

les **billes (f.)** (lay-bee) marbles 34

les **biscuits (m.)** (lay-bee-skwee) cookies 35

le **blanc** (luh-blA^n) white 30

la **blessure** (lah-bleh-sUR) injury 58

les **blettes (f.)** (lay-blet) chard 10

le **bleu clair** (luh-bluh-kleR) light blue 30

le **bleu foncé** (luh-bluh-fO^n-say) dark blue 30

le **blouson** (luh-bloo-zO^n) jean jacket 23

boire (bwahR) to drink 24

le **bois à brûler** (luh-bwah-ah-bRU-lay) firewood 45

la **boîte à pharmacie** (lah-bwah-tah-fahR-mah-see) medicine cabinet 16

la **boîte aux lettres** (lah-bwah-to-letR) mailbox 53

les **boîtes (f.)** (lay-bwaht) jars 29

le **bol** (luh-buhl) bowl 8

le **bonji** (luh-bO^n-jee) bungee jumping 39

le **bonnet** (luh-buh-nay) hat 23, 57

les **bottes (f.)** (lay-buht) boots 23

la **bouche** (lah-boosh) mouth 19

le **boucher** (luh-boo-shay) butcher 56

la **boucherie** (lah-boo-shRee) butcher's 56

le **bouchon** (luh-boo-shO^n) plug 17

la **bouée** (lah-boo-ay) inner tube 69

le **bouffon** (luh-boo-fO^n) jester 75

les **bougeoirs (m.)** (lay-boo-jwahR) candlesticks 72

la **bougie** (lah-boo-jee) candle 7

la **boule** (lah-bool) ball 41; bubble 73

la **boule de verre** (lah-bool-duh-veR) crystal ball 72

le **bouquet de fleurs** (luh-boo-kay-duh-flERR) bunch of flowers 70

la **boussole** (lah-boo-suhl) compass 71

la **bouteille** (lah-boo-tay) bottle 7

le **bouton** (luh-boo-tO^n) button 21

boutonné (boo-tuh-nay) buttoned 26

boutonner (boo-tuh-nay) to button 49

la **boutonnière** (lah-boo-tuh-nyeR) buttonhole 21

le **bracelet** (luh-bRah-slay) bracelet 35

le **brancard** (luh-bRA^n-kahR) stretcher 58

la **branche** (lah-bRA^{n}sh) branch 70

le **bras** (luh-bRah) arm 18

la **brique** (lah-bReek) carton 8

les **briques en plastique** (lay-bRee-kA^n-plah-steek) Lego blocks 54

bronzée (bRO^n-zay) tan 79

la **brosse** (lah-bRuhs) broom 12

la **brosse à cheveux** (lah-bRuh-sah-shuh-vuh) hairbrush 17

la **brosse à dents** (lah-bRuh-sah-dA^n) toothbrush 17

la **brosse à ongles** (lah-bRuh-sah-O^{n}gl) nailbrush 17

brosser (bRuh-say) to brush 25

la **brouette** (lah-bRoo-et) wheelbarrow 61

le **buffet** (luh-bU-fay) sideboard 15

le **bureau** (luh-bU-Ro) desk 14

le **but** (luh-bUt) goal 34

la **cabine téléphonique** (lah-kah-been-tay-lay-fuh-neek) phone booth 53

le **cabinet** (luh-kah-bee-nay) office 58

les **cabinets (m.)** (lay-kah-bee-nay) toilet 16

les **cacahouètes (f.)** (lay-kah-kah-ooet) peanuts 10

le **cache-cache** (luh-kahsh-kahsh) hide-and-seek 34

les **cachets (m.)** (lay-kah-shay) pills 59

le **cactus** (luh-kahk-tUs) cactus 13

le **caddie** (luh-kah-dee) shopping cart 57

le **cadeau** (luh-kah-do) present 6

le **cadre** (luh-kahdR) frame 12

la **cafetière** (lah-kahf-tyeR) coffeemaker 9

la **caisse à outils** (lah-keh-sah-oo-tee) toolbox 13

la **caisse chinoise** (lah-kes-shee-nwahz) Chinese box 42

la **caisse enregistreuse** (lah-kes-A^n-Re-jees-tRuhz) cash register 55

la **caissière** (lah-keh-syeR) cashier 57

le **caleçon** (luh-kahl-sO^n) underpants 22

le **caméscope** (luh-kah-may-skuhp) camcorder 61

le **camion** (luh-kah-myO^n) truck 62

camper (luh-kA^n-peR) to camp 76

le **camping** (luh-kA^n-peeng) camping 70

le **canapé** (luh-kah-nah-pay) sofa 14

le **canard** (luh-kah-nahR) duck 44

le **candélabre** (luh-kA^n-day-lahbR) candleholder 12

le **caniveau** (luh-kah-nee-vo) drain 52

la **canne** (lah-kahn) walking stick 40

la **canne à pêche** (lah-kah-nah-pesh) fishing rod 71

le **canoë** (luh-kah-nuh-ay) canoe 63

le **canoë-kayak** (luh-kah-nuh-ay-kah-yahk) canoeing 39

la **carafe** (lah-kah-Rahf) pitcher 7; bottle 70

caresser (kah-Re-say) to pet 24

la **carotte** (lah-kah-Ruht) carrot 10

le **carré** (luh-kah-Ray) square 30

la **carte** (lah-kahRt) map 29

les **cartes (f.)** (lay-kahRt) cards 34

le **casque** (luh-kahsk) helmet 53

la **casquette** (lah-kah-sket) cap 69

le **casse-tête** (luh-kahs-tet) puzzle 54

les **castagnettes (f.)** (lay-kahs-tah-nyet) castanets 42

le **cd** (luh-say-day) CD 13

le **cerceau** (luh-seR-so) hoop 37

le **cercle** (luh-seRkl) circle 30

les **céréales (f.)** (lay-say-Ray-ahl) cereal 8

le **cerf-volant** (luh-seR-vuh-lA^n) kite 68

la **cerise** (lah-suh-Reez) cherry 7

la **chaîne** (lah-shen) chain 41

la **chaîne hi-fi** (lah-shen-ee-fee) stereo 13

la **chaise** (lah-shez) chair 14

la **chaise-bébé** (lah-shez-bay-bay) high chair 8

la **chaise longue** (lah-shez-lO^{n}g) deck chair 68

la **chaise pliante** (lah-shez-plee-A^{n}t) folding chair 68

la **chambre** (lah-shA^{n}bR) bedroom 20

le **chameau** (luh-shah-mo) camel 47

le **champ** (luh-shA^n) field 70

le **champignon** (luh-shA^n-pee-nyO^n) mushroom 40

le **chanteur** (luh-shA^n-tERR) singer 72

charger (shahR-jay) to load 65

le **chariot** (luh-shah-Ryo) cart 61

le **chariot de nettoyage** (luh-shah-Ryo-duh-ne-twah-yahj) cleaner's cart 60

la **charrette** (lah-shah-Ret) trailer 72

le **chat** (luh-shah) cat 72

le **château** (luh-shah-to) castle 68

le **château gonflable** (luh-shah-to-gO^n-flahbl) inflatable castle 72

chaud (sho) hot 26

le **chauffe-eau** (luh-sho-fo) water heater 9

chaussé (sho-say) with shoes on 27

la **chaussée** (lah-sho-say) road 53

les **chaussettes (f.)** (lay-sho-set) socks 22

les **chaussures (f.)** (lay-sho-sUR) shoes 23

la **chauve-souris** (lah-shov-soo-Ree) bat 41

le **chemin** (luh-shuh-mI^n) path 41

la **cheminée** (lah-shuh-mee-nay) chimney 45

la **chemise** (lah-shuh-meez) shirt 22; folder 21

la **chemise de nuit** (lah-shuh-meez-duh-nwee) nightgown 21

la **chenille** (lah-shuh-nee) caterpillar 71

le **cheval** (luh-shuh-vahl) horse 44

le **cheval d'arçon** (luh-shuh-vahl-dahR-sO^n) vaulting horse 37

le **cheval de voltige** (luh-shuh-vahl-duh-vuhl-teej) vaulting box 37

le **chevalet** (luh-shuh-vah-lay) easel 29

le **chevalier** (luh-shuh-vahl-yay) knight 75

la **cheville** (lah-shuh-vee) ankle 18

la **chèvre** (lah-shevR) goat 44

le **chien** (luh-shyI^n) dog 45

le **chiffon** (luh-shee-fO^n) cloth 12

le **chimpanzé** (luh-shI^n-pA^n-zay) chimpanzee 47

le **chiot** (luh-shyo) puppy 45

les **chips (m.)** (lay-sheeps) potato chips 73

le **chronomètre** (luh-kRo-no-metR) stopwatch 37

la **cible** (lah-seebl) bull's-eye 73

les **cils (m.)** (lay-seel) eyelashes 19

le **cimetière** (luh-seem-tyeR) cemetery 41

le **cinéma** (luh-see-nay-mah) movie theater 52

cinq (sI^{n}k) five 33

le **cinquième** (luh-sI^n-kyee-m) fifth 33

les **ciseaux (m.)** (lay-see-zo) scissors 29

le **citron** (luh-see-tRO^n) lemon 11

la **citrouille** (lah-see-tRoo-ee) pumpkin 10

la **clarinette** (lah-klah-Ree-net) clarinet 43

le **classeur** (luh-klah-sERR) binder 29

le **clavier** (luh-klahv-yay) keyboard 13

la **clé** (lah-klay) key 13

la **clochette** (lah-kluh-shet) handbell 40

la **clôture** (lah-klo-tUR) fence 70

clouer (kloo-ay) to nail 77

les **clous (m.)** (lay-kloo) nails 13

le **clown** (luh-kloon) clown 72

la **coccinelle** (lah-kuhk-see-nel) ladybug 71

le **cochon** (luh-kuh-shO^n) pig 45

le **cochon de lait** (luh-kuh-shO^n-duh-lay) piglet 45

le **code à barres** (luh-kuh-dah-bahR) bar code 57

le **cœur** (luh-kERR) heart 30, 58

le **coffre** (luh-kuhfR) trunk 20

coiffé (kwah-fay) combed 27

la **coiffeuse** (lah-kwah-fuhz) dressing table 15

le **coin** (luh-kwI^n) corner 12

le **collant** (luh-kuh-lA^n) tights 22

la **colle** (lah-kuhl) glue 29

le **collier** (luh-kuhl-yay) necklace 35

colorier (kuh-luh-Ryay) to color 48

la **commode** (lah-kuh-muhd) dresser 15

compter (kO^n-tay) to count 48
le comptoir (luh-kO^n-twahR) counter 56
la conductrice (lah-kO^n-dUk-tRees) driver 53
conduire (kO^n-dweeR) to drive 64
confortable (kO^n-fuhR-tahbl) comfortable 27
les congas (f.) (lay-kO^n-gah) conga drums 42
les conserves (f.) (lay-kO^n-seRv) canned food 57
la consigne (lah-kO^n-see-nyuh) luggage locker 61
construire (kO^ns-tRUeeR) to build 76
le conte (luh-kO^nt) story 21
le conteneur (luh-kO^n-tuh-nERR) container 57
content (kO^n-tA^n) happy 27
la contrebasse (lah-kO^ntR-bahs) double bass 42
le contrôleur (luh-kO^n-tRo-lERR) (ticket) collector 60
le coq (luh-kuhk) rooster 45
la coquille (lah-kuh-kee) shell 69
le cor (luh-kuhR) French horn 43
la corbeille à papier (lah-kuhR-bay-ah-pah-pyay) wastepaper bin 29
la corde (lah-kuhRd) jump rope 34; rope 70
la corde à nœuds (lah-kuhR-dah-nuh) rope 36
le cornet (luh-kuhR-nay) cornet (trumpet) 43; ice-cream cone 69
le corps (luh-kuhR) body 18
le coton (luh-kuh-tO^n) cotton 59
les coton-tiges (m.) (lay-kuh-tO^n-teej) cotton swabs 17
le cou (luh-koo) neck 19
la couche (lah-koosh) diaper 20
le coude (luh-kood) elbow 19
coudre (koodR) to sew 49
la couette (lah-koo-et) comforter 20; ponytail 34
couler (koo-lay) to sink 76
les couleurs (f.) (lay-koo-lERR) colors 30
coupée (koo-pay) cut 66
couper (koo-pay) to cut 48
le couple (luh-koopl) couple 73
courageux (koo-Rah-juh) brave 79
la courgette (lah-kooR-jet) zucchini 10
courir (koo-ReeR) to run 76
la couronne (lah-koo-Ruhn) crown 7
la course (lah-kooRs) race 39
courts (kooR) short 50
le cousin (luh-koo-zI^n) cousin 7
le coussin (luh-koo-sI^n) cushion 12
le couteau (luh-koo-to) knife 9
le couteau de poche (luh-koo-to-duh-puhsh) penknife 70
le couvercle (luh-koo-veRkl) lid 8
la couverture (lah-koo-veR-tUR) blanket 20
le couvre-lit (luh-koovR-lee) bedspread 20
le cow-boy (luh-ko-buhy) cowboy 74
le crabe (luh-kRahb) crab 69
les craies (f.) (lay-kRay) pieces of chalk 28
le crâne (luh-kRahn) skull 58
le crapaud (luh-kRah-po) toad 45
le crayon (luh-kRay-O^n) pencil 29
la crème solaire (lah-kRem-so-leR) sunscreen 69
creuser (kRuh-zay) to dig 77
la crinière (lah-kRee-nyeR) mane 44
le croissant de lune (luh-kRwah-sA^n-duh-lUn) half moon 30
les crotales (m.) (lay-kRo-tahl) small cymbals 41
crues (kRU) raw 66
le cube (luh-kUb) cube 37
la cuillère (lah-kwee-yeR) spoon 9

la cuisine (lah-kwee-zeen) kitchen 8
cuisiner (kwee-zee-nay) to cook 24
la cuisinière (lah-kwee-zee-nyeR) cook 74
la cuisse (lah-kwees) thigh 19
la culotte (lah-kU-luht) panties 22
les cure-dents (m.) (lay-kUR-dA^n) toothpicks 7
curieux (kU-Ryuhz) curious 67
la cuvette (lah-kU-vet) laundry basket 12
le cyclisme (luh-see-kleesm) cycling 38

les dalles (f.) (lay-dahl) tiles 16
les dames (f.) (lay-dahm) checkers 55
la danseuse (lah-dA^n-suhz) ballet dancer 74
le dard (luh-dahR) dart 73
de (duh) from 51
déballer (day-bah-lay) to unwrap 48
debout (duh-boo) standing 50
déboutonné (day-boo-tuh-nay) unbuttoned 26
déboutonner (day-boo-tuh-nay) to unbutton 49
la décapotable (day-kah-puh-tahbl) convertible 68
décembre (day-sA^nbR) December 32
décharger (day-shahR-jay) to unload 65
décoiffé (day-kwah-fay) uncombed 27
décoller (day-kuh-lay) to take off 64
dedans (duh-dA^n) in 51
dégonflée (day-gO^n-flay) deflated 78
les déguisements (m.) (day-geez-mA^n) costumes 74
déguster (day-gUs-tay) to taste 24
dehors (duh-uhR) out 51
le deltaplane (luh-del-tah-plahn) hang gliding 39
dénouer (day-noo-ay) to untie 49
le dentifrice (luh-dA^n-tee-fRees) toothpaste 17
les dents (f.) (lay-dA^n) teeth 19
le déodorant (luh-day-o-duh-RA^n) deodorant 17
dépasser (day-pah-say) to pass 65
dernier (deR-nyay) last 79
derrière (deR-RyeR) behind 51
descendre (day-sA^ndR) to go down 64
deshabillé (day-zah-bee-yay) undressed 27
dessiner (day-see-nay) to draw 48
les dessins (m.) (lay-day-sI^n) drawings 29
deux (duh) two 33
le deuxième (luh-duh-zyem) second 33
devant (duh-vA^n) in front of 51
la devineresse (lah-duh-vee-nuh-Res) fortune-teller 72
le diable (luh-dyabl) devil 75
différents (dee-fay-RA^n) different 79
difficile (dee-fee-seel) difficult 78
le dimanche (luh-dee-mA^nsh) Sunday 32
le dindon (luh-dI^n-dO^n) turkey 45
le dinosaure (luh-dee-nuh-suhR) dinosaur 21
dire au revoir (deeR-o-RvwahR) to say good-bye 65
distraite (dees-tRet) distracted 50
le distributeur (luh-dees-tRee-bU-tERR) ATM 53
le divan (luh-dee-vA^n) divan 14
dix (dees) ten 33
le dixième (luh-dee-zyem) tenth 33
les doigts (m.) (lay-dwah) fingers 19
domestique (duh-mes-teek) domestic 79
les dominos (m.) (lay-duh-mee-no) dominoes 54
donner le coup de pied (duh-nay-luh-koo-duh-pyay) to kick 49
dormir (duhR-meeR) to sleep 25

le dos (luh-do) back 19
douce (doos) soft 66
la douche (lah-doosh) shower 16
le dragon (luh-dRah-gO^n) dragon 40
le drap (luh-dRah) sheet 20
le drapeau (luh-dRah-po) flag 53
droit (dRwah) straight 26
le dromadaire (dRuh-mah-deR) dromedary 47
dur (dUR) hard 67

l'eau (f.) (lo) water 34
l'eau de cologne (f.) (lo-duh-kuh-luh-nyuh) cologne 16
l'écharpe (f.) (lay-shahRp) scarf 57
les échecs (m.) (lay-zay-shek) chess 55
l'échelle (f.) (lay-shel) ladder 20; window ladder 36
éclabousser (ay-klah-boo-say) to splash 76
éclairer (ay-klay-Ray) to light 49
écouter (ay-koo-tay) to listen 24, 48
l'écran (m.) (lay-kRA^n) screen 13
écrire (ay-kReeR) to write 48
l'écurie (f.) (lay-kU-Ree) stable 44
effacer (ay-fah-say) to erase 48
l'effaceur (m.) (lay-fah-sERR) eraser 29
l'église (f.) (lay-gleez) church 52
l'égouttoir (m.) (lay-goo-twahR) plate rack 9
l'éléphant (m.) (lay-lay-fA^n) elephant 46
les élèves (m. or f.) (lay-zay-lev) students 28
embrasser (A^n-bRah-say) to kiss 24
en bas (A^n-bah) down 51
en désordre (A^n-day-zuhR-dRuh) messy 26
en face (A^n-fahs) opposite 51
en haut (A^n-o) up 51
en ordre (A^n-uhRdR) neat 26
endormi (A^n-duhR-mee) asleep 27
ennuyée (A^n-nwee-yay) bored 67
enrhumé (A^n-RU-may) with a cold 67
ensoleillé (A^n-suh-lay-yay) sunny 78
entière (A^n-tyeR) whole 66
entre (A^ntR) between 51
entrer (A^n-tRay) to go in 64
entrer en collision (A^n-tRay-A^n-kuh-lee-zyO^n) to crash 65
envelopper (A^n-vluh-pay) to wrap 48
épaisse (ay-pes) thick 66
l'épaule (f.) (lay-pol) shoulder 19
l'épée (f.) (lay-pay) sword 41
épicé (ay-pee-say) spicy 66
les épices (f.) (lay-zay-pees) spice rack 8
l'épingle à cheveux (f.) (lay-pI^ngl-ah-shuh-vuh) barrette 35
éplucher (ay-plU-shay) to peel 24
l'éponge (f.) (lay-pO^nj) sponge 17
épousseter (ay-poos-tay) to clean 25
l'épouvantail (m.) (ay-poo-vA^n-tai) scarecrow 71
l'équitation (f.) (lay-kee-tah-syO^n) horseback riding 38
escalader (es-kah-lah-day) to climb 77
l'escalier d'incendie (m.) (les-kahl-yay-dI^n-sA^n-dee) fire escape 53
l'escargot (m.) (les-kahR-go) snail 71
l'escrime (f.) (les-kReem) fencing 39
l'espalier (m.) (les-pahl-yay) wall bars 36
l'estomac (m.) (les-tuh-mah) stomach 58
l'étable (f.) (lay-tahbl) barn 44
étaler (ay-tah-lay) to spread (out) 24
l'été (m.) (lay-tay) summer 32
éteinte (ay-tI^nt) off 26
étendre (ay-tA^ndR) to hang up 25
éternuer (ay-teR-nU-ay) to sneeze 65
étiré (ay-tee-Ray) ironed 26; 78

l'étoile (f.) (lay-twahl) star 30
étrange (ay-tRAnj) strange 79
étroit (ay-tRwah) narrow 78
éveillé (ay-vay-yay) awake 27
l'évier (m.) (lay-vyay) sink 9
l'excavatrice (f.) (leks-kah-vah-tRees) excavator 62
l'excursion (f.) (leks-kUR-syOn) trip 44
expliquer (eks-plee-kay) to explain 48
l'extincteur (m.) (leks-tInk-tERR) fire extinguisher 37
l'extracteur (m.) (leks-tRahk-tERR) range hood 8

facile (fah-seel) easy 78
le facteur (luh-fahk-tERR) mail carrier 53
faible (febl) weak 50
faire cadeau (feR-kah-do) to give a present 24
faire de la bicyclette (feR-duh-lah-bee-see-klet) to ride a bicycle 64
faire de la plongée (feR-duh-lah-plOn-jay) to dive 76
faire la pirouette (feR-lah-pee-Roo-et) to turn somersaults 49
faire son lit (feR-sOn-lee) to make one's bed 25
le fait-tout (luh-fuh-too) casserole 9
la famille (lah-fah-mee) family 6
le fanion (luh-fah-nyOn) banner 57
le fantôme (luh-fAn-tom) ghost 40
fatiguée (fah-tee-gay) tired 50
le fauteuil (luh-fo-tuhy) armchair 14
le fauteuil à bascule (luh-fo-tuhy-ah-bahs-kUl) rocking chair 14
le fauteuil roulant (luh-fo-tuhy-Roo-lAn) wheelchair 34
la fée (lah-fay) fairy 40
la femme de nettoyage (lah-fahm-duh-net-wah-yahj) cleaner 60
la femme policier (lah-fahm-puh-lee-syay) policewoman 74
la femme préhistorique (lah-fahm-pRay-ees-tuh-Reek) cavewoman 75
la fenêtre (lah-fuh-netR) window 9, 61
le fer à repasser (luh-feR-ah-Ruh-pah-say) iron 13
la ferme (lah-feRm) farm 44
fermé (feR-may) closed 26, 66; with the lid on 67
fermer (feR-may) to close 64
la fermeture éclair (lah-feR-muh-tUR-ay-kleR) zipper 21
le fermier (luh-feRm-yay) farmer 44
féroce (fay-Ruhs) fierce 79
le feu (luh-fuh) traffic light 53
la feuille (lah-fuhy) sheet of paper 28
les feuilles (f.) (lay-fuhy) leaves 70
le feutre (luh-fuhtR) marker 29
février (fay-vRee-yay) February 32
fine (feen) thin 66
flairer (flay-Ray) to sniff 77
la flaque (lah-flahk) puddle 52
flotter (fluh-tay) to float 76
les flotteurs (m.) (lay-fluh-tERR) floats 69
la flûte (lah-flUt) recorder 43
la flûte indienne (lah-flUt-In-dyen) panpipes 43
la flûte traversière (lah-flUt-tRah-veR-syeR) flute 43
fondre (fOndR) to melt 76
la fontaine (lah-fOn-ten) water fountain 34
le football (luh-foot-bol) soccer 38
les formes (f.) (lay-fuhRm) shapes 30

fort (fuhR) strong 50
la foudre (lah-foodR) bolt of lightning 41
le foulard (luh-foo-lahR) scarf 57
le four (luh-fooR) oven 8
le four micro-ondes (luh-fooR-mee-kRo-Ond) microwave 8
la fourchette (lah-fooR-shet) fork 9
le fourgon (luh-fooR-gOn) freight car 61
la fourgonnette (lah-fooR-guh-net) van 62
les fourmis (f.) (lay-fooR-mee) ants 71
fragile (fRah-jeel) fragile 78
les fraises (f.) (lay-fRez) strawberries 11
les franges (f.) (lay-fRAnj) tassles 13
freiner (fRay-nay) to brake 65
le frère (luh-fReR) brother 6
le frigo (luh-fRee-go) fridge 9
frisés (fRee-zay) curly 50
frites (fReet) fried 66
la friteuse (lah-fRee-tuhz) fryer 9
froid (fRwah) cold 26
le front (luh-fROn) forehead 19
les fruits (m.) (lay-fRwee) fruit 10, 56
la fumée (lah-fU-may) smoke 70
la fusée (lah-fU-zay) rocket 63

les gants (m.) (lay-gAn) gloves 57
le garde-manger (luh-gahRd-mAn-jay) hutch 15
garder (gahR-day) to guard 65
le gardien (luh-gahR-dyIn) goalie 34
la gare (lah-gahR) train station 60
les gâteaux (m.) (lay-gah-to) cakes 53
gâtée (gah-tay) spoiled 66
la gaze (lah-gahz) gauze bandage 58
le gel (luh-jel) shower gel 16
la génisse (lah-jay-nees) calf 45
le genou (luh-juh-noo) knee 19
la genouillière (lah-juh-nooy-yeR) knee pad 36
le gilet (luh-jee-lay) vest 22
le gilet de sauvetage (luh-jee-lay-duh-sov-tahj) life jacket 69
la gimblette (lah-jIn-blet) doughnut 7
la girafe (lah-jee-Rahf) giraffe 46
la girouette (lah-jee-Roo-et) weather vane 45
la glâce à l'eau (lah-glahs-ah-lo) ice-cream pop 69
le glaçon (luh-glah-sOn) ice cube 7
glisser (glee-say) to slip 64
le golf (luh-guhlf) golf 38
la gomme (lah-guhm) eraser 29
gonflée (gOn-flay) inflated 78
le gorille (luh-guh-Ree) gorilla 47
la gourde (lah-gooRd) water bottle 71
gourmande (gooR-mAnd) greedy 67
grande (gRAnd) big 26, 50
la grand-mère (lah-gRAn-meR) grandmother 6
le grand-père (luh-gRAn-peR) grandfather 6
la grande roue (lah-gRAnd-Roo) Ferris wheel 72
le grelot (luh-gRuh-lo) bell 72
grelotter (gRuh-luh-tay) to shiver 76
le grenat (luh-gRuh-nah) maroon 30
le grenier à foin (luh-gRuh-nyay-ah-fwIn) hayloft 45
griffer (gRee-fay) to scratch 77
la grille (lah-gRee) railings 34
le grille-pain (luh-gRee-pIn) toaster 9
gris (gRee) gray 30
gros (gRo) fat 50
guérir (gay-ReeR) to cure 65
la guitare (lah-gee-tahR) guitar 42

la guitare électrique (lah-gee-tahR-ay-lek-tReek) electric guitar 42
le gymnase (luh-jeem-nahz) gym 36

habillé (ah-bee-yay) dressed 27
la hache (lah-ahsh) axe 45
le hamac (luh-ah-mahk) hammock 70
le hamburger (luh-Am-booR-geR) hamburger 73
le hand-ball (luh-And-bol) handball 38
les haricots verts (m.) (lay-ah-Ree-ko-veR) green beans 10
l'harmonica (m.) (lahR-muh-nee-kah) harmonica 43
le hautbois (luh-o-bwah) oboe 43
le haut-de-forme (luh-o-duh-fuhRm) top hat 73
le haut-parleur (luh-o-pahR-lERR) stereo speaker 13; loudspeaker 60
l'hélicoptère (m.) (lay-lee-kuhp-teR) helicopter 63
l'herbe (f.) (leRb) grass 71
l'hippopotame (m.) (lee-puh-puh-tahm) hippopotamus 46
l'hiver (m.) (lee-veR) winter 32
le hochet (luh-uh-shay) baby's rattle 21
le hockey (luh-uh-kay) hockey 38
le hot-dog (m.) (luh-uht-duhg) hot dog 73
l'hôtel (m.) (lo-tel) hotel 52
la houe (lah-oo) hoe 45
huit (weet) eight 33
la huitième (luh-wee-tyem) eighth 33

l'île (f.) (leel) island 69
les images (f.) (lay-zee-mahj) pictures 35
l'imperméable (m.) (lIn-peR-may-ahbl) raincoat 23
incommode (In-kuh-muhd) uncomfortable 27
l'index (m.) (lIn-deks) index finger 19
l'infirmière (f.) (lIn-feeR-myeR) nurse 58
l'information (f.) (lIn-fuhR-mah-syOn) information desk 60
les instruments à clavier (m.) (lay-zIns-tRU-mAn-ah-klah-vyay) keyboard instruments 43
les instruments à cordes (m.) (lay-zIns-tRU-mAn-ah-kuhRd) string instruments 42
les instruments à percussion (m.) (lay-zIns-tRU-mAn-ah-peR-kU-syOn) percussion instruments 42
les instruments à vent (m.) (lay-zIns-tRU-mAn-ah-vAn) wind instruments 43
les instruments de musique (m.) (lay-zIns-sRU-mAn-duh-mU-zeek) musical instruments 42
l'interrupteur (m.) (lIn-teR-RUp-tERR) electric switch 13

la jambe (lah-jAnb) leg 18
janvier (jAn-vyay) January 32
le jardinier (luh-jahR-dee-nyay) gardener 34
la jardinière (lah-jahR-dee-nyeR) window box 35
le jaune (luh-jon) yellow 30
jeter (juh-tay) to throw 49
le jeu des petits chevaux (m.) (luh-juh-day-puh-tee-shuh-vo) Parcheesi 55
le jeu vidéo (luh-juh-vee-day-o) video game 55
le jeudi (luh-juh-dee) Thursday 32
jeune (juhn) young 50
les jeux (m.) (lay-juh) games 54

joindre (jwIⁿdR) to join 48
les jointures des doigts (f.) (lay-jwIⁿ-tUR-day-dwah) knuckles 19
le jongleur (luh-jOⁿ-glERR) juggler 72
jouer (joo-ay) to play 48; to perform 49
jouer d'un instrument (joo-ay-duhn-Iⁿs-tRU-mAⁿ) to play an instrument 48
les jouets (m.) (lay-joo-ay) toys 54
le journal (luh-jooR-nahl) newspaper 61
les jours (m.) (lay-jooR) days 32
juillet (jwee-ay) July 32
juin (jwIⁿ) June 32
les jumelles (f.) (lay-jU-mel) binoculars 61
la jument (lah-jU-mAⁿ) mare 44
la jupe (lah-jUp) skirt 22
le jus (luh-jU) juice 8
jusque (jUs-kuh) up to 51
le justaucorps (luh-jUs-to-cuhR) leotard 36

le kangourou (luh-kAⁿ-goo-Roo) kangaroo 47
le kiosque (luh-kee-uhsk) kiosk 68
le kiwi (luh-kee-wee) kiwi 11
le koala (luh-kuh-ah-lah) koala 47

labourer (lah-boo-Ray) to plow 77
le lac (luh-lahk) lake 71
les lacets (m.) (lay-lah-say) laces 21
lâche (lahsh) cowardly 79
lâcher (lah-shay) to let go of 49
laid (lay) ugly 50
la laitue (lay-tU) lettuce 10
le lama (luh-lah-mah) llama 46
la lampe (lah-lAⁿp) lamp 12; reading lamp 20
la lampe de poche (lah-lAⁿp-duh-puhsh) flashlight 41
le lampion (luh-lAⁿ-pyOⁿ) paper lantern 72
la langue (lah-lAⁿg) tongue 19
la langue de belle-mère (lah-lAⁿg-duh-bel-meR) noisemaker 7
le lapereau (luh-lah-pRo) bunny 44
le lapin (luh-lah-pIⁿ) rabbit 44
large (lahRj) wide 78
le lavabo (luh-lah-vah-bo) sink 17
laver (lah-vay) to wash 24
le lave-vaisselle (luh-lahv-ves-sel) dishwasher 9
lécher (lay-shay) to lick 77
les légumes (m.) (lay-lay-gUm) vegetables 10
lente (lAⁿt) slow 78
le léopard (luh-lay-o-pahR) leopard 46
les lettres (f.) (lay-letR) letters 28
les lèvres (f.) (lay-levR) lips 19
le lézard (luh-lay-zahR) lizard 71
la libellule (lah-lee-bel-lUl) dragonfly 71
libre (leebR) free 67, 78
le lion (luh-lyOⁿ) lion 46
liquide (lee-keed) liquid 66
lire (leeR) to read 48
le lit (luh-lee) bed 15
le livre (luh-leevR) book 13
loin (lwIⁿ) far 51
longs (lOⁿ) long 50
la loupe (lah-loop) magnifying glass 70
la luette (lah-lU-et) uvula 19
le lundi (luh-lIⁿ-dee) Monday 32
la lune (lah-lUn) moon 40
les lunettes (f.) (lay-lU-net) eyeglasses 35
les lunettes de plongée (f.) (lay-lU-net-duh-plOⁿ-jay) goggles 69
les lunettes de soleil (f.) (lay-lU-net-duh-suh-lay) sunglasses 69

le lutin (luh-lU-tIⁿ) elf 41
le lynx (luh-lIⁿks) lynx 46

la machine à laver (lah-mah-shee-nah-lah-vay) washing machine 9
le magasin (luh-mah-gah-zIⁿ) store 52
le magicien (luh-mah-jee-syIⁿ) magician 72
le magnétoscope (luh-mah-nyay-tuh-skuhp) video recorder 13
mai (may) May 32
le maillot de bain (luh-mai-yo-duh-bIⁿ) swimming trunks 23; swimsuit 23
la main (lah-mIⁿ) hand 18
le majeur (luh-mah-jERR) middle finger 19
mal élevée (mah-layl-vay) bad-mannered 79
malade (mah-lahd) sick 67
le manège (luh-mah-nej) merry-go-round 72
la mangeoire (lah-mAⁿ-jwahR) trough 44
manger (mAⁿ-jay) to eat 24
la mangue (lah-mAⁿg) mango 11
le manteau (luh-mAⁿ-to) coat 23
maquiller (mah-kee-yay) to make up 49
les maracas (f.) (lay-mah-Rah-kah) maracas 42
le marchand de fruits (luh-mahR-shAⁿ-duh-fRwee) fruit stall 56
marcher (mahR-shay) to walk 76
le mardi (luh-mahR-dee) Tuesday 32
la mare (lah-mahR) pond 45
la marionnette (lah-mah-Ryo-net) puppet 73
les marionnettes (f.) (lay-mah-Ryo-net) puppets 55
la marmelade (lah-mahR-muh-lahd) jam 9
le marron (luh-mah-ROⁿ) brown 30
mars (mahRs) March 32
le marteau (luh-mahR-to) hammer 13
le masque (luh-mahsk) mask 7, 58, 72
le matelas (luh-mah-tlah) mattress 20; air bed 68
le mauve (luh-mov) purple 30
le mécanicien (luh-may-kah-nee-syIⁿ) engine driver 60
la mécanicienne (lah-may-kah-nee-syen) mechanic 74
la médaille (lah-may-dai) medal 35
le médecin (luh-mayd-sIⁿ) doctor 58
les médicaments (m.) (lay-may-dee-kah-mAⁿ) medicine 58
le melon (luh-muh-lOⁿ) melon 11
le menton (luh-mAⁿ-tOⁿ) chin 19
la mer (lah-meR) sea 63, 69
le mercredi (luh-meR-kRuh-dee) Wednesday 32
la mère (lah-meR) mother 6
le métro (luh-may-tRo) subway 53
les meubles (m.) (lay-muhbl) furniture 14
le micro (luh-mee-kRo) microphone 73
les miettes (f.) (lay-myet) crumbs 52
le mil (luh-meel) club 36
mince (mIⁿs) thin 50
la minerve (lah-mee-neRv) surgical collar 73
le miroir (luh-mee-RwahR) mirror 17
le mixeur (luh-mee-ksERR) blender 9
modeler (muh-dlay) to shape 48
moderne (muh-deRn) modern 66
les mois (m.) (lay-mwah) months 32
moissonner (mwah-suh-nay) to mow 77
les molaires (f.) (lay-muh-leR) molars 19
le mollet (luh-muh-lay) calf (of leg) 19
le monstre (luh-mOⁿstR) monster 40
la montagne (lah-mOⁿ-tah-nyuh) mountain 70
les montagnes russes (f.) (lay-mOⁿ-tah-nyuh-RUs) roller coaster 72
monter (mOⁿ-tay) to go up 64

la montre (lah-mOⁿtR) watch 37
montrer (mOⁿ-tRay) to point (out) 76
le monument (luh-muh-nU-mAⁿ) memorial 52
la moto (lah-mo-to) motorcycle 62
la moto nautique (lah-mo-to-no-teek) jet ski 68
mou (moo) soft 67
les mouchoirs en papier (m.) (lay-moo-shwahR-Aⁿ-pah-pyay) tissues 17
les moufles (f.) (lay-moofl) mittens 57
mouillée (moo-yay) wet 27
le moule (luh-mool) mold 69
le moulin (luh-moo-lIⁿ) windmill 44
le mousquetaire (luh-mous-kuh-teR) musketeer 75
la moustache (lah-moos-tash) moustache 40
le mouton (luh-moo-tOⁿ) sheep 45
les moyens (m.) (lay-mwah-yIⁿ) means 62
le mur (luh-mUR) wall 13
mûre (mUR) ripe 66
les muscles (m.) (lay-mUskl) muscles 58

la nappe (lah-nahp) tablecloth 6
la natation (lah-nah-tah-syOⁿ) swimming 38
le navet (luh-nah-vay) turnip 10
naviguer (nah-vee-gay) to sail 76
la nèfle (lah-nefl) medlar 11
la neige (lah-nej) snow 70
le néon (luh-nay-Oⁿ) fluorescent light 37
nerveuse (neR-vuhz) nervous 67
nettoyer (net-wah-yay) to mop 25
neuf (nuhf) new 26; nine 33
le neuvième (luh-nuh-vyem) ninth 33
le nez (luh-nay) nose 19
le nid (luh-nee) nest 71
le noir (luh-nwahR) black 30
les noisettes (f.) (lay-nwah-zet) hazelnuts 10
les noix (f.) (lay-nwah) walnuts 11
la noix de coco (lah-nwah-duh-ko-ko) coconut 11
le nombril (luh-nOⁿ-bRee) belly button 18
normale (nuhR-mahl) normal 79
novembre (nuh-vAⁿbR) November 32
le nuage (luh-nU-ahj) cloud 68
nuageux (nU-ah-juh) cloudy 78
les numéros (m.) (lay-nU-may-Ro) numbers 33

observer (uhp-seR-vay) to watch 76
occupée (uh-kU-pay) busy 67
l'ocre (m.) (luhkR) ochre 30
octobre (uhk-tuhbR) October 32
l'oie (f.) (lwah) goose 45
l'oignon (m.) (luh-nyOⁿ) onion 10
les oiseaux (m.) (lay-zwah-zo) birds 70
l'ongle (m.) (lOⁿgl) fingernail 19
l'opticien (m.) (luhp-tee-syIⁿ) optician's 53
l'orange (f.) (luh-RAⁿj) orange (fruit) 11; orange (color) 30
l'orang-outan (m.) (luh-RAⁿ-oo-tAⁿ) orangutan 47
l'ordinateur (m.) (luhR-dee-nah-tERR) computer 13
l'oreille (f.) (luh-Ray) ear 19
l'oreiller (m.) (luh-Ray-yay) pillow 20
l'orgue (m.) (luhRg) organ 43
l'oncle (m.) (lOⁿkl) uncle 6
l'os (m.) (luhs) bone 71
l'ours brun (m.) (looRs-bRIⁿ) brown bear 47
l'ours panda (m.) (looRs-pAⁿ-dah) panda bear 47
l'ours polaire (m.) (looRs-puh-leR) polar bear 47

ouvert (oo-veR) open 26, 66
l'ouvreuse (f.) (loo-vRuhz) usher 40
l'ouvrier (m.) (loo-vRee-yay) worker 61
ouvrir (oo-vReeR) to open 64
l'ovale (m.) (lo-vahl) oval 30

la paille (lah-pai) straw 6
le palais (luh-pah-lay) palate 19
pâle (pahl) pale 79
le pamplemousse (luh-pA^{n}pl-moos) grapefruit 11
le panier (luh-pah-nyay) basket 34, 57
la panne (lah-pahn) breakdown 52
le panneau (luh-pah-no) road sign 53
le panneau coulissant (luh-pah-no-koo-lee-sA^n) partition 16
le panneau d'affichage (luh-pah-no-dah-fee-shahj) information board 60
le pansement (luh-pA^{n}s-mA^n) Band-Aid 58
le pantalon (luh-pA^n-tah-lO^n) pants 23
la panthère (lah-pA^n-teR) panther 46
le papier hygiénique (luh-pah-pyay-eej-yay-neek) toilet paper 16
le papillon (luh-pah-pee-yO^n) butterfly 71
le parapluie (luh-pah-Rah-plwee) umbrella 61
le parasol (luh-pah-Rah-suhl) awning 53; beach umbrella 68
le parc (luh-pahRk) park 52
le pare-chocs (luh-pahR-shuhk) bumper 53
pareilles (pah-Ray) alike 79
paresseux (pah-Res-suh) lazy 67
le parfum (luh-pahR-fI^n) perfume 16
parler (pahR-lay) to speak 48
parler au téléphone (pahR-lay-o-tay-lay-fuhn) to talk on the phone 64
les parties (f.) (lay-pahR-tee) parts 18
la passoire (lah-pah-swahR) strainer 9
la pastèque (lah-pahs-tek) watermelon 11
la pâte à modeler (lah-pah-tah-muh-dlay) clay 29
le patient (luh-pah-syA^n) patient 58
le patinage (luh-pah-tee-nahj) skating 38
la patinette (lah-pah-tee-net) scooter 54
les patins (m.) (lay-pah-tI^n) skates 54
la paupière (lah-po-pyeR) eyelid 19
le paysage (luh-pay-zahj) landscape 12
la pêche (lah-pesh) peach 11
pêcher (pay-shay) to fish 77
le pêcheur (luh-pay-shERR) fisherman 71
le pédalo (luh-pay-dah-lo) pedal boat 69
le peigne (luh-pe-nyuh) comb 17
le peignoir (luh-pe-nywahR) bathrobe 16
peindre (pI^{n}dR) to paint 77
le peintre (luh-pI^{n}tR) painter 74
la pelle (lah-pel) dustpan 13; shovel 69
la pelote (lah-puh-luht) ball 29
la peluche (lah-puh-lUsh) teddy bear 54
la pendule (lah-pA^n-dUl) clock 6
la perceuse (lah-peR-suhz) drill 13
le père (luh-peR) father 6
la perruque (lah-peR-RUk) wig 72
la persienne (lah-peR-syen) blinds 12
peser (puh-zay) to weigh 65
le petit avion (luh-puh-tee-tah-vyO^n) light aircraft 63
le petit cheval de bois (luh-puh-tee-shuh-vahl-duh-bwah) rocking horse 55
le petit doigt (luh-puh-tee-dwah) pinky (finger) 19
le petit garçon (luh-puh-tee-gahR-sO^n) boy 29
petite (puh-teet) small 26; short 50
la petite cuillère (lah-puh-teet-kwee-yeR) teaspoon 9

la petite fille (lah-puh-teet-fee) girl 29
les petits pois (m.) (lay-puh-tee-pwah) peas 10
le phare (luh-fahR) lighthouse 69
la photo (lah-fo-to) photograph 28
la photographe (lah-fo-to-gRahf) photographer 74
le piano (luh-pyah-no) piano 43
le pic (luh-peek) pick 61
les pièces (f.) (lay-pyes) coins 57
le pied (luh-pyay) foot 18
pieds nus (pyay-nU) barefoot 27
la pierre (lah-pyeR) stone 70
les pigeons (m.) (lay-pee-jO^n) pigeons 52
le pilote (luh-pee-luht) race driver 74
la pince (lah-pI^{n}s) pliers 13
le pinceau (luh-pI^n-so) paintbrush 29
le ping-pong (luh-pee-nyuh-pO^{n}g) ping-pong 39
la pique (lah-peek) pike 36
piquer (pee-kay) to sting, to break up 77
le pirate (luh-pee-Raht) pirate 75
la pirouette (lah-pee-Roo-et) somersault 37
les pistaches (f.) (lay-pees-tahsh) pistachio nuts 10
les places (f.) (lay-plahs) seats 40
le plafond (luh-plah-fO^n) ceiling 12
la plage (lah-plahj) beach 68
la planche à couper (lah-plA^{n}sh-ah-koo-pay) cutting board 8
la planche à repasser (lah-plA^{n}sh-ah-Ruh-pah-say) ironing board 12
la planche à roulettes (lah-plA^{n}sh-ah-Roo-let) skateboard 54
la planche à voile (lah-plA^{n}sh-ah-vwahl) windsurfing 39
la plante (lah-plA^{n}t) plant 6
la plaque (lah-plahk) license plate 53
le plateau (luh-plah-to) tray 8
le plâtre (luh-plahtR) cast 59
plein (plI^n) full 26
pleurer (pluh-Ray) to cry 65
plié (plee-ay) folded 78
plissé (plee-say) wrinkled 26
la plume (plUm) feather 41
le plumeau (luh-plU-mo) feather duster 13
le pneu (luh-pnuh) tire 53
la poêle (lah-pwahl) frying pan 9
le poêlon (luh-pwah-lO^n) saucepan 8
la poignée (lah-pwah-nyay) (door) knob 17
le poignet (luh-pwah-nyay) wrist 19
la poire (lah-pwahR) pear 11
le poireau (luh-pwah-Ro) leek 10
le poisson (luh-pwah-sO^n) fish 56, 70
la poissonnière (lah-pwah-suh-nyeR) fishmonger 56
la poitrine (lah-pwah-tReen) breast/chest 18
le poivron rouge (luh-pwah-vRO^n-Rooj) red pepper 10
le poivron vert (luh-pwah-vRO^n-veR) green pepper 10
le polo (luh-puh-lo) knitted shirt 22
la pommade (lah-puh-mahd) ointment 59
la pomme (lah-puhm) apple 11
la pomme de terre (lah-puhm-duh-teR) potato 10
la pompe à essence (lah-pO^n-pah-es-sA^{n}s) gas pump 68
le pompier (luh-pO^n-pyay) fireman 74
le pont (luh-pO^n) bridge 68
le pop-corn (luh-puhp-kuhRn) popcorn 73
la porcherie (lah-puhR-shRee) pigsty 44
la porte (lah-puhRt) door 12
le porte-clés (luh-puhRt-klay) key ring 13
le portefeuille (luh-puhRt-fuhl) wallet 57

le portemanteau (luh-puhRt-mA^n-to) hanger 21; clothes rack 28
le porte-monnaie (luh-puhRt-muh-nay) coin purse 57
le portrait (luh-puhR-tRay) portrait 12
la poste (lah-puhst) post office 52
le poste de radio (luh-puhst-duh-Rah-dyo) radio 16
le poster (luh-puhs-teR) poster 20
le pot de fleurs (luh-po-duh-flERR) flowerpot 35
les pots (m.) (lay-po) jars 8
les pots de peinture (m.) (lay-po-duh-pI^n-tUR) paints 28
la poubelle (lah-poo-bel) garbage can 9
le pouce (luh-poos) thumb 19
le pouf (luh-poof) ottoman 14
le poulain (luh-poo-lI^n) pony 44
les poules (f.) (lay-pool) hens 44
le poumon (luh-poo-mO^n) lung 58
la poupée (lah-poo-pay) doll 55
le poupon (luh-poo-pO^n) doll 21
pousser (poo-say) to push 49
les pousses (f.) (lay-poos) shoots 28
la poussette (lah-poo-set) (baby) stroller 57
les poussins (m.) (lay-poo-sI^n) chicks 44
la poutre (lah-pootR) beam (ceiling) 44
la première (lah-pRuh-myeR) first 33
première (pRuh-myeR) first 79
prendre dans ses bras (pRA^{n}dR-dA^n-say-bRah) to hug 24
prendre le bain (pRA^{n}dR-luh-bI^n) to take a bath 25
prendre le soleil (pRA^{n}dR-luh-suh-lay) to sunbathe 76
près (pRay) near 51
le presse-citron (luh-pRes-see-tRO^n) juicer 9
le prince (luh-pRI^{n}s) prince 41
le printemps (luh-pRI^n-tA^n) spring 32
la prise de courant (lah-pReez-duh-koo-RA^n) electric socket 13
prisonnière (pRee-zuh-nyeR) caught 78
le professeur (luh-pRuh-fes-sERR) teacher 28
les projecteurs (m.) (lay-pRuh-jek-tERR) spotlights 40
propre (pRuhpR) clean 27
le pull-over (luh-pU-luh-veR) sweater 22
le pulvérisateur (luh-pUl-vay-Ree-zah-tERR) spray bottle 13
le puma (luh-pU-mah) puma 46
le puzzle (luh-puhzl) jigsaw puzzle 54
le pyjama (luh-pee-jah-mah) pajamas 20

le quai (luh-kay) platform 61
quatre (kahtR) four 33
le quatrième (luh-kah-tRee-yem) fourth 33
la queue (lah-kuh) line 34
les quilles (f.) (lay-kee) bowling 55

le radiocassette (luh-Rah-dyo-kah-set) radio cassette (player) 21
la radiographie (lah-Rah-dyo-gRah-fee) x-ray 58
le rafraîchissement (luh-Rah-fRay-shees-mA^n) soft drink 73
le rafting (luh-Rahf-tee-nyuh) rafting 39
raides (Red) straight 50
le rail (luh-Rai) rail 61
les raisins (m.) (lay-Ray-zI^n) grapes 11
les raisins secs (m.) (lay-Ray-zI^n-sek) raisins 11
ramer (Rah-may) to row 76
la rampe (lah-RA^{n}p) ramp 35; banister 35

ramper (RAⁿ-pay) to slither 76
la randonnée (lah-RAⁿ-duh-nay) hiking 39
rapide (Rah-peed) fast 78
la raquette (lah-Rah-ket) racket 20
le rasoir (luh-Rah-zwahR) razor 17
le râteau (luh-Rah-to) rake 45
rayer (Ray-yay) to cross out 48
rebondir (Ruh-bOⁿ-deeR) to bounce 49
le rectangle (luh-Rek-tAⁿgl) rectangle 30
la règle (lah-Regl) ruler 29
les rênes (lay-Ren) reins 45
repasser (Ruh-pah-say) to iron 25
résistante (Ray-zees-tAⁿt) resistant 78
respirer (Res-pee-Ray) to breathe 65
le réveil (luh-Ray-vay) alarm clock 21
le réverbère (luh-Ray-veR-beR) lamppost 53
le rhinocéros (luh-Ree-nuh-say-Ruhs) rhinoceros 46
le rideau (luh-Ree-do) curtain 9, 41
rire (ReeR) to laugh 65
la rivière (lah-Ree-vyeR) river 70
la robe (lah-Ruhb) dress 22
la robe chasuble (lah-Ruhb-shah-sUbl) jumper 22
la robe de chambre (lah-Ruhb-duh-shAⁿbR) housecoat 21
le robinet (luh-Ruh-bee-nay) faucet 17
le robot (luh-Ruh-bo) robot 20
le roi (luh-Rwah) king 75
rompre (ROⁿpR) to break 24
la ronde (lah-ROⁿd) circle 35
le rose (luh-Roz) pink (color) 30
la roue (lah-Roo) wheel 53
le rouge (luh-Rooj) red 30
le rouge à levres (luh-Roo-jah-levR) lipstick 17
le rouleau (luh-Roo-lo) rolling pin 9
le rouleau de papier (luh-Roo-lo-duh-pah-pyay) paper towels 9
le ruban (luh-RU-bAⁿ) ribbon 35, 36
la ruche (lah-RUsh) beehive 70
le rugby (luh-RUg-bee) rugby 38
rugueuse (RU-guhz) rough 66

le sable (luh-sahbl) sand 69
le sac (luh-sahk) bag 6; purse 57; sack 61
le sac à dos (luh-sah-kah-do) backpack 28
sain (sIⁿ) healthy 67
les saisons (f.) (lay-say-zOⁿ) seasons 32
sale (sahl) dirty 27
salé (sah-lay) salty 66
la salière (lah-sah-lyeR) saltshaker 7
la salle d'attente (lah-sahl-dah-tAⁿt) waiting room 59
la salle de bains (lah-sahl-duh-bIⁿ) bathroom 16
la salle de séjour (lah-sahl-duh-say-jooR) living room 12
la salopette (lah-sah-luh-pet) overalls 23
saluer (sah-lU-ay) to greet 49
le samedi (luh-sahm-dee) Saturday 32
les sandales (f.) (lay-sAⁿ-dahl) sandals 23
le sandwich (luh-sAⁿd-weesh) sandwich 7
sans couvercle (sAⁿ-koo-veRkl) with the lid off 67
le saut en hauteur (luh-so-Aⁿ-o-tERR) high jump 39
le saut en longueur (luh-so-Aⁿ-lOⁿ-gERR) long jump 39
le saut des haies (luh-so-day-hay) hurdle jump 39
sauter (so-tay) to jump 49
sauvage (so-vahj) wild 79
les savates (f.) (lay-sah-vaht) flip-flops 68
le savon (luh-sah-vOⁿ) soap 17

le saxophone (luh-sahk-suh-fuhn) saxophone 43
la scène (lah-sen) stage 40
le scientifique (luh-see-yAⁿ-tee-feek) scientist 74
scier (see-yay) to saw 77
le scotch (luh-skuhtsh) tape 29
se cacher (suh-kah-shay) to hide 49
se coucher (suh-koo-shay) to go to bed 25
se couper les ongles (suh-koo-pay-lay-zOⁿgl) to cut one's nails 25
se doucher (suh-doo-shay) to take a shower 76
s'étirer (say-tee-Ray) to stretch 25
se laver (suh-lah-vay) to wash oneself 25
se lever (suh-luh-vay) to get up 25
se mettre de la crème (suh-metR-duh-lah-kRem) to put cream on 76
se moucher (suh-moo-shay) to blow one's nose 65
se peigner (suh-pen-yay) to comb one's hair 25
se promener (suh-pRuhm-nay) to stroll 64
se raser (suh-Rah-zay) to shave 25
se salir (suh-sah-leeR) to get dirty 25
se sécher (suh-say-shay) to dry oneself 25
le seau (luh-so) bucket 69
sèche (sesh) dry 27
le séchoir (luh-say-shwahR) hair dryer 17
le secouriste (luh-suh-koo-Reest) lifeguard 68
le secrétaire (luh-suh-kRay-teR) desk 15
la selle (lah-sel) saddle 45
la semaine (lah-suh-men) week 32
semer (suh-may) to sow 77
sentir (sAⁿ-teeR) to smell 24
séparer (say-pah-Ray) to separate 48
sept (set) seven 33
septembre (sep-tAⁿ-bR) September 32
le septième (luh-se-tyem) seventh 33
la seringue (lah-suh-RIⁿg) syringe 59
le serpent (luh-seR-pAⁿ) snake 47
le serpentin (luh-seR-pAⁿ-tIⁿ) paper streamer 6
le serre-tête (luh-seR-tet) headband 35
la serviette (lah-seR-vyet) napkin 6
la serviette de bain (lah-seR-vyet-duh-bIⁿ) towel 17
servir (seR-veeR) to serve 24
le shampoing (luh-shAⁿ-pwIⁿ) shampoo 16
le short (luh-shoRt) shorts 23
le siège (luh-syej) seat 59
le sifflet (luh-see-flay) whistle 35
le sirop (luh-see-Ro) syrup 59
six (sees) six 33
le sixième (luh-see-zyem) sixth 33
le ski (luh-skee) skiing 38
le snowboard (luh-sno-buhRd) snowboarding 39
la sœur (lah-sERR) sister 6
le soldat (luh-suhl-dah) soldier 75
le soleil (luh-suh-lay) sun 68
solide (suh-leed) solid 66
la sonnaille (lah-suh-nai) bell 45
la sorcière (lah-suhR-syeR) witch 41
la sortie (lah-suhR-tee) exit 40
sortir (suhR-teeR) to go out 64
souffler (soo-flay) to blow 24
le sourcil (luh-sooR-see) eyebrow 19
la souris (lah-soo-Ree) mouse 13, 75
sous (soo) under 51
le sparadrap (luh-spah-Rah-dRah) medical tape 58
les spectateurs (m.) (lay-spek-tah-tERR) spectators 40
les sports (m.) (lay-spuhR) sports 38

le squelette (luh-skuh-let) skeleton 72
la station-service (lah-stah-syOⁿ-seR-vees) gas station 68
le stéthoscope (luh-stay-tuh-skuhp) stethoscope 59
le store (luh-stuhR) roller blind 6
le stylo (luh-stee-lo) pen 29
sucer (sU-say) to lick 77
la sucette (lah-sU-set) (baby's) pacifier 21
sucré (sU-kRay) sweet 66
le sucrier (luh-sU-kRee-yay) sugar bowl 9
suer (sU-ay) to sweat 49
la sueur (lah-sU-ERR) sweat 36
le sultan (luh-sUl-tAⁿ) sultan 75
le superhéros (luh-sU-peR-ay-Ro) superhero 75
le supermarché (luh-sU-peR-mahR-shay) supermarket 56
sur (sUR) on 51
les surgelés (m.) (lay-sUR-juh-lay) frozen food 57
le survêtement (luh-sUR-vet-mAⁿ) tracksuit 36

la table (lah-tahbl) dining table 14
la table de nuit (lah-tahbl-duh-nwee) nightstand 21
la table ronde (lah-tahbl-ROⁿd) round table 14
le tableau (luh-tah-blo) blackboard 29
les tableaux (m.) (lay-tah-blo) paintings 12
le tablier (luh-tah-blee-yay) apron 56
le tabouret (luh-tah-boo-Ray) stool 16
la taille (lah-tai) waist 19
le taille-crayon (luh-tai-kRay-Oⁿ) pencil sharpener 29
tailler (tai-yay) to sharpen 48; to prune 77
le talc (luh-tahlk) talcum powder 17
le talkie-walkie (luh-to-kee-wo-kee) walkie-talkie 54
le talon (luh-tah-lOⁿ) heel 19
le tambour (luh-tAⁿ-booR) drum 42
le tambourin (luh-tAⁿ-boo-RIⁿ) tambourine 41, 42
la tante (lah-tAⁿt) aunt 7
le tapis (luh-tah-pee) rug 13
le tapis de sol (luh-tah-pee-duh-suhl) mat 36
le tapis de souris (luh-tah-pee-duh-soo-Ree) mousepad 13
la tarte (lah-tahRt) cake 6
la tasse (lah-tahs) cup 9
le taureau (luh-tuh-Ro) bull 45
le taxi (luh-tahk-see) taxi 62
le tee-shirt (luh-tee-shERRt) T-shirt 22
le téléphone portable (luh-tay-lay-fuhn-puhR-tahbl) mobile phone 53
la télévision (lah-tay-lay-vee-zyOⁿ) television 12
le temps (luh-tAⁿ) time 32
les tenailles (f.) (lay-tuh-nai) pincers 13
tenir (tuh-neeR) to hold 49
le tennis (luh-ten-nees) tennis 38
la tente (lah-tAⁿt) tent 70
la terre (lah-teR) land 62
la tête (lah-tet) head 19
téter (tay-tay) to suckle 77
le théâtre (luh-tay-ahtR) theater 40
le thermomètre (luh-teR-muh-metR) thermometer 59
le thermos (luh-teR-mos) thermos 71
le tibia (luh-tee-byah) shin 19
le tigre (luh-teegR) tiger 46
la timbale (lah-tIⁿ-bahl) kettle drum 42
le tir à cible (luh-teeR-ah-seebl) target shooting 73

PHRASES

ENGLISH-FRENCH GLOSSARY

accordion l'accordéon (m.) 43
air l'air (m.) 63
air bed le matelas 68
alarm clock le réveil 21
album l'album (m.) 35
alcohol l'alcool (m.) 58
alike pareilles 79
almonds les amandes (f.) 10
alphabet l'alphabet (m.) 31
ambulance l'ambulance (f.) 62
angel l'ange (m.) 75
animals les animaux (m.) 46
ankle la cheville 18
ants les fourmis (f.) 71
apple la pomme 11
apricot l'abricot (m.) 11
April avril 32
apron le tablier 56
arm le bras 18
armchair le fauteuil 14
armoire l'armoire (f.) 15
around autour 51
artichoke l'artichaut (m.) 10
asleep endormi 27
asparagus les asperges (f.) 10
astronaut l'astronaute (m. or f.) 74
ATM le distributeur 53
to attack attaquer 77
attentive attentive 50
August août 32
aunt la tante 7
autumn/fall l'automne (m.) 32
avocado l'avocat (m.) 11
awake éveillé 27
awning le parasol 53
axe la hache 45

baby le bébé 6
baby's bottle le biberon 21
baby's rattle le hochet 21
back le dos 19
backpack le sac à dos 28
bad-mannered mal élevée 79
bag le sac 6
balconies les balcons (m.) 52
ball le ballon 21, 34; la pelote 29; la boule 41
ballet dancer la danseuse 74
balloons les ballons (m.) 6
banana la banane 11
to bandage bander 65
bandage la bande 59
Band-Aid le pansement 58
banister la rampe 35
banjo le banjo 42
bank la banque 53
banner le fanion 57
bar la barre 9
bar code le code à barres 57
barbecue le barbecue 70
barefoot pieds nus 27
barn l'étable (f.) 44
barrel le tonneau 45
barrette l'épingle à cheveux (f.) 35
barrier la barrière 61
baseball le base-ball 38

basket le panier 34, 57
basketball le basket-ball 38
bassoon le basson 43
bat la chauve-souris 41
bath la baignoire 16
bathrobe le peignoir 16
bathroom la salle de bains 16
bathrooms les toilettes (f.) 59
beach la plage 68
beach umbrella le parasol 68
beam (ceiling) la poutre 44
beard la barbe 40
bed le lit 15
bedroom la chambre 20
bedspread le couvre-lit 20
bee l'abeille (f.) 70
beehive la ruche 70
behind derrière 51
bell la sonnaille 45; le grelot 72
belly button le nombril 18
bench le banc 52
between entre 51
bib le bavoir 8
bicycle la bicyclette 54
bidet le bidet 16
big grande 26
binder le classeur 29
binoculars les jumelles (f.) 61
birds les oiseaux (m.) 70
bitter amer 66
black le noir 30
blackboard le tableau 29
blanket la couverture 20
blender le mixeur 9
blinds la persienne 12
to blow souffler 24
to blow one's nose se moucher 65
boat la barque 69
body le corps 18
bolt of lightning la foudre 41
bone l'os (m.) 71
book le livre 13
bookcase la bibliothèque 15
boots les bottes (f.) 23
bored ennuyée 67
bottle la bouteille 7; la carafe 70
to bounce rebondir 49
bowl le bol 8
bowling les quilles (f.) 55
boy le petit garçon 29
bracelet le bracelet 35
braids les tresses (f.) 35
to brake freiner 65
branch la branche 70
brave courageux 79
to break rompre 24
to break up piquer 77
breakdown la panne 52
breast/chest la poitrine 18
to breathe respirer 65
bridge le pont 68
broom la brosse 12; le balai 41
brother le frère 6
brown le marron 30
brown bear l'ours brun (m.) 47
to brush brosser 25
bubble la boule 73

bucket le seau 69
to build construire 76
bull le taureau 45
bull's-eye la cible 73
bumper le pare-chocs 53
bunch of flowers le bouquet de fleurs 70
bungee jumping le bonji 39
bunny le lapereau 44
bus l'autobus (m.) 62
bus stop l'arrêt de bus (m.) 52
busy occupée 67
butcher le boucher 56
butcher's la boucherie 56
butterfly le papillon 71
to button boutonner 49
button le bouton 21
buttoned boutonné 26
buttonhole la boutonnière 21

cactus le cactus 13
cake la tarte 6
cakes les gâteaux (m.) 53
calf la génisse 45
calf (of leg) le mollet 19
calm tranquille 67
camcorder le caméscope 61
camel le chameau 47
camera l'appareil photo (m.) 60
to camp camper 76
camping le camping 70
candle la bougie 7
candleholder le candélabre 12
candlesticks les bougeoirs (m.) 72
candy cane le bâton à bonbon 73
canned food les conserves (f.) 57
canoe le canoë 63
canoeing le canoë-kayak 39
cap la casquette 69
car la voiture 53, 55, 62
cardigan la veste 22
cards les cartes (f.) 34
carrot la carotte 10
cart le chariot 61
carton la brique 8
case la trousse 28
cash register la caisse enregistreuse 55
cashew nuts les anacardes (m.) 10
cashier la caissière 57
casserole le fait-tout 9
cast le plâtre 59
castanets les castagnettes (f.) 42
castle le château 68
cat le chat 72
caterpillar la chenille 71
caught prisonnière 78
cavewoman la femme préhistorique 75
CD le cd 13
ceiling le plafond 12
cello le violoncelle 42
cemetery le cimetière 41
cereal les céréales (f.) 8
chain la chaîne 41
chair la chaise 14
chard les blettes (f.) 10
checkers les dames (f.) 55
cherry la cerise 7

chess les échecs (m.) 55
chicks les poussins (m.) 44
chimney la cheminée 45
chimpanzee le chimpanzé 47
chin le menton 19
Chinese box la caisse chinoise 42
to chop down abattre 77
church l'église (f.) 52
circle le cercle 30; la ronde 35
clarinet la clarinette 43
clay la pâte à modeler 29
to clean épousseter 25
clean propre 27
cleaner la femme de nettoyage 60
cleaner's cart le chariot de nettoyage 60
to climb escalader 77
climbing l'alpinisme (m.) 39
clock la pendule 6
to close fermer 64
closed fermé 26, 66
cloth le chiffon 12
clothes les vêtements (m.) 22
clothes rack le portemanteau 28
cloud le nuage 68
cloudy nuageux 78
clown le clown 72
club le mil 36
coat le manteau 23
coconut la noix de coco 11
coffeemaker la cafetière 9
coin purse le porte-monnaie 57
coins les pièces (f.) 57
cold froid 26
cologne l'eau de cologne (f.) 16
to color colorier 48
colors les couleurs (f.) 30
comb le peigne 17
to comb one's hair se peigner 25
combed coiffé 27
comfortable confortable 27
comforter la couette 20
comic (strip) la bande dessinée 35
compass la boussole 71
computer l'ordinateur (m.) 13
conga drums les congas (f.) 42
container le conteneur 57
convertible la décapotable 68
to cook cuisiner 24
cook la cuisinière 74
cookies les biscuits (m.) 35
corner le coin 12
cornet (trumpet) le cornet 43
costumes les déguisements (m.) 74
cotton le coton 59
cotton candy la barbe à papa 73
cotton swabs les coton-tiges (m.) 17
to cough tousser 65
to count compter 48
counter le comptoir 56
couple le couple 73
cousin le cousin 7
cow la vache 45
cowardly lâche 79
cowboy le cow-boy 74
crab le crabe 69
to crash entrer en collision 65
crawling tunnel le tunnel 36
crib le berceau 15, 20
crooked tordu 26
to cross traverser 64
to cross out rayer 48
crown la couronne 7
crumbs les miettes (f.) 52
crutch la béquille 35
to cry pleurer 65
crystal ball la boule de verre 72

cube le cube 37
cup la tasse 9
to cure guérir 65
curious curieux 67
curly frisés 50
curtain le rideau 9, 41
cushion le coussin 12
to cut couper 48
cut coupée 66
to cut one's nails se couper les ongles 25
cutting board la planche à couper 8
cycling le cyclisme 38

dark blue le bleu foncé 30
dark green le vert foncé 30
dart le dard 73
days les jours (m.) 32
December décembre 32
deck chair la chaise longue 68
deflated dégonflée 78
deodorant le déodorant 17
desk le bureau 14; le secrétaire 15
devil le diable 75
diaper la couche 20
different différents 79
difficult difficile 78
to dig creuser 77
dining table la table 14
dinosaur le dinosaure 21
dirty sale 27
dishwasher le lave-vaisselle 9
display cabinet la vitrine 15
distracted distraite 50
divan le divan 14
to dive faire de la plongée 76
doctor le médecin 58
dog le chien 45
doll le poupon 21, 55
domestic domestique 79
dominoes les dominos (m.) 54
donkey l'âne (m.) 45
door la porte 12
(door) knob la poignée 17
double bass la contrebasse 42
doughnut la gimblette 7
down en bas 51
to drag traîner 49
dragon le dragon 40
dragonfly la libellule 71
drain le caniveau 52
drawer le tiroir 21
drawings les dessins (m.) 29
dress la robe 22
dressed habillé 27
dresser la commode 15
dressing table la coiffeuse 15
drill la perceuse 13
to drink boire 24
to drive conduire 64
driver la conductrice 53
dromedary le dromadaire 47
to draw dessiner 48
drum le tambour 42
drum set la batterie 42
dry sèche 27
to dry oneself se sécher 25
duck le canard 44
dustpan la pelle 13

ear l'oreille (f.) 19
easel le chevalet 29
easy facile 78
to eat manger 24
eight huit 33

eighth la huitième 33
elbow le coude 19
electric guitar la guitare électrique 42
electric socket la prise de courant 13
electric switch l'interrupteur (m.) 13
elephant l'éléphant (m.) 46
elf le lutin 41
empty vide 26
engine driver le mécanicien 60
to erase effacer 48
eraser l'effaceur (m.) 29; la gomme 29
excavator l'excavatrice (f.) 62
exit la sortie 40
to explain expliquer 48
eyebrow le sourcil 19
eyeglasses les lunettes (f.) 35
eyelashes les cils (m.) 19
eyelid la paupière 19
eyes les yeux (m.) 19

fairy la fée 40
family la famille 6
far loin 51
farm la ferme 44
farmer le fermier 44
fast rapide 78
fat gros 50
father le père 6
faucet le robinet 17
feather la plume 41
feather duster le plumeau 13
February février 32
fence la clôture 70
fencing l'escrime (f.) 39
Ferris wheel la grande roue 72
field le champ 70
fierce féroce 79
fifth le cinquième 33
fingernail l'ongle (m.) 19
fingers les doigts (m.) 19
fire engine la voiture de pompiers 62
fire escape l'escalier d'incendie (m.) 53
fire extinguisher l'extincteur (m.) 37
fireman le pompier 74
firewood le bois à brûler 45
first la première 33, première 79
to fish pêcher 77
fish le poisson 56, 70
fisherman le pêcheur 71
fishing rod la canne à pêche 71
fishmonger la poissonnière 56
five cinq 33
flag le drapeau 53
flashlight la lampe de poche 41
flip-flops les savates (f.) 68
to float flotter 76
floats les flotteurs (m.) 69
flock of sheep le troupeau 71
flowerpot le pot de fleurs 35
fluorescent light le néon 37
flute la flûte traversière 43
to fly voler 76
folded plié 78
folder la chemise 21
folding chair la chaise pliante 68
foot le pied 18
footprints les traces (f.) 68
forearm l'avant-bras (m.) 19
forehead le front 19
fork la fourchette 9
fortune-teller la devineresse 72
four quatre 33
fourth le quatrième 33
fragile fragile 78
frame le cadre 12

magic wand la baguette magique 41
magician le magicien 72
magnet l'aimant (m.) 9
magnifying glass la loupe 70
mail carrier le facteur 53
mailbox la boîte aux lettres 53
to make one's bed faire son lit 25
to make up maquiller 49
mane la crinière 44
mango la mangue 11
map la carte 29
maracas les maracas (f.) 42
marbles les billes (f.) 34
March mars 32
mare la jument 44
marker le feutre 29
maroon le grenat 30
martial arts les arts martiaux (m.) 39
mask le masque 7, 58, 72
mat le tapis de sol 36
matches les allumettes (f.) 7
mattress le matelas 20
May mai 32
means les moyens (m.) 62
meat la viande 56
mechanic la mécanicienne 74
medal la médaille 35
medical tape le sparadrap 58
medicine les médicaments (m.) 58
medicine cabinet la boîte à pharmacie 16
medlar la nèfle 11
melon le melon 11
to melt fondre 76
memorial le monument 52
merry-go-round le manège 72
messy en désordre 26
microphone le micro 73
microwave le four micro-ondes 8
middle finger le majeur 19
mirror le miroir 17
mittens les moufles (f.) 57
mobile phone le téléphone portable 53
modern moderne 66
molars les molaires (f.) 19
mold le moule 69
Monday le lundi 32
monster le monstre 40
months les mois (m.) 32
moon la lune 40
to mop nettoyer 25
mother la mère 6
motorcycle la moto 62
mountain la montagne 70
mouse la souris 13, 75
mousepad le tapis de souris 13
moustache la moustache 40
mouth la bouche 19
movie theater le cinéma 52
to mow moissonner 77
muscles les muscles (m.) 58
mushroom le champignon 40
musical instruments les instruments de musique (m.) 42
musketeer le mousquetaire 75

to nail clouer 77
nailbrush la brosse à ongles 17
nails les clous (m.) 13
napkin la serviette 6
narrow étroit 78
near près 51
neat en ordre 26
neck le cou 19
necklace le collier 35
neighbor le voisin 7, la voisine 7

nervous nerveuse 67
nest le nid 71
new neuf 26
newspaper le journal 61
next to à côté de 51
nightgown la chemise de nuit 21
nightstand la table de nuit 21
nine neuf 33
ninth le neuvième 33
noisemaker la langue de belle-mère 7
normal normale 79
nose le nez 19
November novembre 32
numbers les numéros (m.) 33
nurse l'infirmière (f.) 58

oboe le hautbois 43
ochre l'ocre (m.) 30
October octobre 32
off éteinte 26
office le cabinet 58
ointment la pommade 59
old vieux 26, 50; ancien 66
on allumée 26; sur 51
one un 33
onion l'oignon (m.) 10
to open ouvrir 64
open ouvert 26, 66
opposite en face 51
optician's l'opticien (m.) 53
orange (color) l'orange (m.) 30
orange (fruit) l'orange (f.) 11
orangutan l'orang-outan (m.) 47
organ l'orgue (m.) 43
ottoman le pouf 14
out dehors 51
oval l'ovale (m.) 30
oven le four 8
overalls la salopette 23

pacifier la sucette 21
to paint peindre 77
paintbrush le pinceau 29
painter le peintre 74
paintings les tableaux (m.) 12
paints les pots de peinture (m.) 28
pajamas le pyjama 20
palate le palais 19
pale pâle 79
panda bear l'ours panda (m.) 47
panpipes la flûte indienne 43
panther la panthère 46
panties la culotte 22
pants le pantalon 23
paper lantern le lampion 72
paper streamer le serpentin 6
paper towels le rouleau de papier 9
parallel bars les barres parallèles (f.) 37
Parcheesi le jeu des petits chevaux 55
park le parc 52
partition le panneau coulissant 16
parts les parties (f.) 18
to pass dépasser 65
passenger car le wagon de passagers 61
path le chemin 41
patient le patient 58
peach la pêche 11
peanuts les cacahouètes (f.) 10
pear la poire 11
peas les petits pois (m.) 10
pedal boat le pédalo 69
to peel éplucher 24
pen (writing) le stylo 29
pen (farm) le bercail 44

pencil le crayon 29
pencil sharpener le taille-crayon 29
penknife le couteau de poche 70
pepper le poivron 10
percussion instruments les instruments à percussion (m.) 42
to perform jouer 49
perfume le parfum 16
to pet caresser 24
phone booth la cabine téléphonique 53
photograph la photo 28
photographer la photographe 74
piano le piano 43
pick le pic 61
pictures les images (f.) 35
pieces of chalk les craies (f.) 28
pig le cochon 45
pigeons les pigeons (m.) 52
piggy bank la tirelire 21
piglet le cochon de lait 45
pigsty la porcherie 44
pike la pique 36
pillow l'oreiller (m.) 20
pills les cachets (m.) 59
pincers les tenailles (f.) 13
pineapple l'ananas (m.) 11
ping-pong le ping-pong 39
pink le rose 30
pinky (finger) le petit doigt 19
pipe la tuyauterie 34
pirate le pirate 75
pistachio nuts les pistaches (f.) 10
pitcher la carafe 7
plane l'avion (m.) 63
plant la plante 6
plate l'assiette (f.) 9
plate rack l'égouttoir (m.) 9
platform le quai 61
to play jouer 48
to play an instrument jouer d'un instrument 48
pliers la pince 13
to plow labourer 77
plug le bouchon 17
to point (out) montrer 76
polar bear l'ours polaire (m.) 47
policewoman la femme policier 74
pond la mare 45
pony le poulain 44
ponytail la couette 34
popcorn le pop-corn 73
portrait le portrait 12
post office la poste 52
poster le poster 20
potato la pomme de terre 10
potato chips les chips (m.) 73
potty le vase de nuit 17
present le cadeau 6
prince le prince 41
to prune tailler 77
puddle la flaque 52
puma le puma 46
pumpkin la citrouille 10
puppet la marionnette 73
puppets les marionnettes (f.) 55
puppy le chiot 45
purple le mauve 30
purse le sac 57
to push pousser 49
to put cream on se mettre de la crème 76
puzzle le casse-tête 54

rabbit le lapin 44
race la course 39
race car la voiture de course 62

sweat la sueur 36
sweater le pull-over 22
to sweep balayer 25
sweet sucré 66
swimming la natation 38
swimming trunks le maillot de bain 23
swimsuit le maillot de bain 23
sword l'épée (f.) 41
syringe la seringue 59
syrup le sirop 59

tablecloth la nappe 6
to take a bath prendre le bain 25
to take a shower se doucher 76
to take off décoller 64
talcum powder le talc 17
to talk on the phone parler au téléphone 64
tall grande 50
tambourine le tambourin 41, 42
tame tranquille 79
tan bronzée 79
tape le scotch 29
target shooting le tir à cible 73
tassles les franges (f.) 13
to taste déguster 24
taxi le taxi 62
teacher le professeur 28
teaspoon la petite cuillère 9
teddy bear la peluche 54
teeth les dents (f.) 19
television la télévision 12
ten dix 33
tennis le tennis 38
tent la tente 70
tenth le dixième 33
theater le théâtre 40
thermometer le thermomètre 59
thermos le thermos 71
thick épaisse 66
thigh la cuisse 19
thin fine 66; mince 50
third le troisième 33
three trois 33
through à travers 51
to throw jeter 49
thumb le pouce 19
Thursday le jeudi 32
ticket collector le contrôleur 60
to tie up attacher 49
tiger le tigre 46
tights le collant 22
tiles les dalles (f.) 16
time le temps 32
tire le pneu 53
tired fatiguée 50
tissues les mouchoirs en papier (m.) 17
toad le crapaud 45
toast le toast 8
toaster le grille-pain 9
toilet les cabinets (m.) 16
toilet paper le papier hygiénique 16
tomato la tomate 10
tongue la langue 19
toolbox la caisse à outils 13
toothbrush la brosse à dents 17
toothpaste le dentifrice 17
toothpicks les cure-dents (m.) 7
top (toy) la toupie 35
top hat le haut-de-forme 73
tortoise la tortue 47
to touch toucher 24
tourist le touriste 60
toward à 51
towel la serviette de bain 17

tower la tour 68
town le village 70
toys les jouets (m.) 54
track la voie 61
tracksuit le survêtement 36
tractor le tracteur 62
traffic light le feu 53
trailer la charrette 72
train le train 62
train station la gare 60
trampoline le trampoline 37
transportation le transport 62
to travel voyager 65
tray le plateau 8
treasure le trésor 40
tree l'arbre (m.) 71
triangle le triangle 30, 41
tricycle le tricycle 54
trip l'excursion (f.) 44
trombone le trombone 43
trough la mangeoire 44
truck le camion 62
trumpet la trompette 43
trunk le coffre 20
T-shirt le tee-shirt 22
tuba le tuba 43
Tuesday le mardi 32
turban le turban 73
turkey le dindon 45
to turn virer 65
to turn somersaults faire la pirouette 49
turnip le navet 10
twig le bâton 70
two deux 33

ugly laid 50
ultralight (aircraft) l'U.L.M. (m.) 63
umbrella le parapluie 61
to unbutton déboutonner 49
unbuttoned déboutonné 26
uncle l'oncle 6
uncombed décoiffé 27
uncomfortable incommode 27
under sous 51
underpants le caleçon 22
undressed deshabillé 27
to unload décharger 65
unripe vert 66
to untie dénouer 49
to unwrap déballer 48
up en haut 51
up to jusque 51
usher l'ouvreuse (f.) 40
uvula la luette 19

vacuum cleaner l'aspirateur (m.) 12
van la fourgonnette 62
vase le vase 12
vaulting box le cheval de voltige 37
vaulting horse le cheval d'arçon 37
vegetables les légumes (m.) 10
vest le gilet 22
video game le jeu vidéo 55
video recorder le magnétoscope 13
viola la viole 42
violin le violon 42
volleyball le volley-ball 38

waist la taille 19
to wait attendre 64
waiting room la salle d'attente 59
to walk marcher 76

walkie-talkie le talkie-walkie 54
walking stick la canne 40
wall le mur 13
wall bars l'espalier (m.) 36
wallet le portefeuille 57
walnuts les noix (f.) 11
to wash laver 24
to wash oneself se laver 25
washing machine la machine à laver 9
wastepaper bin la corbeille à papier 29
to watch observer 76
watch la montre 37
to water arroser 76
water l'eau (f.) 34
water bottle la gourde 71
water fountain la fontaine 34
water heater le chauffe-eau 9
watercolors les aquarelles (f.) 28
watering can l'arrosoir (m.) 69
watermelon la pastèque 11
wave la vague 69
weak faible 50
weather vane la girouette 45
Wednesday le mercredi 32
week la semaine 32
to weigh peser 65
well-mannered bien élevée 79
wet mouillée 27
wheel la roue 53
wheelbarrow la brouette 61
wheelchair le fauteuil roulant 34
to whisk battre 24
whistle le sifflet 35
white le blanc 30
white asparagus les asperges (f.) 10
whole entière 66
wide large 78
wig la perruque 72
wild sauvage 79
wind instruments les instruments à vent (m.) 43
windmill le moulin 44
window la fenêtre 9, 61
window box la jardinière 35
window ladder l'échelle (f.) 36
windsurfing la planche à voile 39
winter l'hiver (m.) 32
witch la sorcière 41
with a cold enrhumé 67
with shoes on chaussé 27
with the lid off sans couvercle 67
with the lid on fermée 67
worker l'ouvrier (m.) 61
to wrap envelopper 48
wrinkled plissé 26
wrist le poignet 19
to write écrire 48

x-ray la radiographie 58
xylophone le xylophone 42

yacht le yacht 63
to yawn bâiller 25
year l'année (f.) 32
yellow le jaune 30
yogurt le yaourt 9
young jeune 50
yo-yo le yo-yo 35

zebra le zèbre 46
zipper la fermeture éclair 21
zucchini la courgette 10